DRIVING ENERGY-EFFICIENT AND LOW-CARBON INVESTMENTS FOR SMALL AND MEDIUM-SIZED ENTERPRISES THROUGH THE FINANCE SECTOR

SEPTEMBER 2024

ASIAN DEVELOPMENT BANK

Notes:
In this publication, "$" refers to United States dollars and "₹" refers to Indian rupees.
ADB recognizes "Bombay" as Mumbai.

Cover design by Claudette Rodrigo.

CONTENTS

TABLES, FIGURES, AND BOXES

Tables

Figures

Boxes

FOREWORD

On behalf of the Asian Development Bank (ADB), it is my pleasure to introduce this report *Driving Energy-Efficient and Low-Carbon Investments for Small and Medium-Sized Enterprises through the Finance Sector*.

The report identifies the manufacturing industry, commercial building, and transport sectors in India with a focus on opportunities to scale the participation of small and medium-sized enterprises in adopting low-carbon technologies. These three sectors account for over two-thirds of the Indian energy consumption. The report presents a detailed assessment of energy savings, greenhouse gas emission reduction potential, and investment requirements.

India has set a target of a net carbon zero economy by 2070. This country-level commitment—along with India's nationally determined contributions—places a clear priority and focus on the significant untapped potential to invest in energy efficiency and electric mobility solutions, among other climate-smart infrastructure (CSI) segments.

Investments in these sectors face different challenges. Many are well-documented and well-known barriers in the energy efficiency financing space ranging from awareness of suitable technologies or access to suitable financing solutions. Most of the interventions by international development agencies and the Government of India have developed and strengthened the basic framework to promote energy efficiency solutions. There are barriers and challenges in the larger-scale deployment of investments in low-carbon technologies across the target sectors.

This report presents a detailed assessment of the market and operational barriers that need to be bridged through innovative financing solutions. Multistakeholder collaboration and innovative solutions are needed to get access to adequate financing suitable to meet the needs of the range of stakeholders in the energy efficiency and low-carbon technology supply chain including energy service companies, small and medium-sized enterprises, original equipment manufacturers, local service providers, electric vehicle manufacturers, as well as other related suppliers of CSI solutions.

The report also presents possible solutions for the different sectors and addresses most of the challenges. It presents the outlook through strengths, weaknesses, opportunities, and threats analysis and provides insights into actionable measures that could be taken to scale the proposed solutions.

Financial institutions, nonbanking financial companies, original equipment manufacturers, energy service companies, industry players, government bodies, and the Reserve Bank of India must work together to ensure that the solutions outlined in the report are fully explored in the direction to support the country's long-term decarbonization goals.

ADB would like to express gratitude to those who generously contributed their time and expertise to enrich this discussion, which helped form the basis for the recommendations for scaling access to finance for the energy efficiency, CSI, and electric mobility sectors in this report. ADB looks forward to working with the Government of India to implement these solutions and others in support of India's net-zero goals.

Suzanne Gaboury
Director General
Private Sector Operations Department
Asian Development Bank

ACKNOWLEDGMENTS

The report *Driving Energy-Efficient and Low-Carbon Investments for Small and Medium-Sized Enterprises through the Finance Sector* was prepared by staff of the Asian Development Bank (ADB) and experts in clean energy financing from PricewaterhouseCoopers Private Limited (PwC) India.

The preparation of this report is supported under the Technical Assistance 6586 IND: Energy Efficiency and Climate-Smart Infrastructure Opportunities for Financial Institutions, phases 1 and 2 (54340-001) and administered by ADB.

The study team would like to thank the Clean Technology Fund for financing this technical assistance project.

This report is prepared under the overall guidance of Susan Olsen, principal investment specialist, Private Sector Financial Institutions Division Unit, Private Sector Operations Department, ADB. Key contributors to the report from ADB's India Resident Mission are Priya Sunder, senior investment officer; Ashley S. Robertson, consultant; Anand Mahadevan, consultant; Nikunj Oli, investment specialist; and Saumadip Dey, senior investment officer.

Energy efficiency and financing experts from PwC India include Amit Kumar (partner, Clean Energy), Kulbhushan Kumar (director), Jayakrishnan P. Nair (associate director), Ameya Subodh (associate director), Amit Seth (senior associate), and Prabhat Sharma (senior associate), who assisted in authoring this report. This report combined secondary research and primary consultations with a select group of stakeholders.

The study also acknowledges the support provided by nonbanking financial companies, financial institutions, energy service companies, original equipment manufacturers, smart infrastructure players, electric mobility (e-mobility) players, and other stakeholders.

Graphic designers and the Printing Services Unit of the Corporate Services Department and the publishing team of the Department of Communications and Knowledge Management at ADB provided support for the publication of this report.

ABOUT THIS STUDY

The Asian Development Bank (ADB) is implementing a technical assistance project to provide support to Indian financial institutions for lending to small and medium-sized enterprises (SMEs) for energy efficiency and climate-smart infrastructure (CSI) initiatives. The technical assistance is consistent with the ADB country partnership strategy for India, 2018–2022, which aims to boost economic competitiveness, address climate change, and provide inclusive access to infrastructure. The strategy states that ADB will work with domestic financial institutions to deepen access to climate finance.

The promotion of energy efficiency and support for CSI technologies are part of ADB's ambition to be the climate bank of Asia and to fund $100 billion in climate finance by 2030.[1] ADB routinely lends to private sector financial institutions in its developing member countries for on-lending to targeted activities with high developmental impact, including enhanced energy efficiency and greenhouse gas emission reduction through CSI.

ADB—through the Private Sector Operations Department—entrusted PricewaterhouseCoopers Private Limited to analyze the market needs for promoting investment in energy efficiency and CSI technologies and to identify private sector financial institutions interested in developing targeted lending programs to help SMEs in India focused on financing for energy efficiency and CSI technologies.

Purpose and Objectives of the Study

The purpose of this study was to outline a comprehensive review of the market landscape for SME investment in energy efficiency and CSI technologies, as well as barriers and opportunities to drive demand for further investments in such measures, primarily in energy-intensive SME industrial sectors, commercial buildings, and electric mobility. The study also intended to provide intelligence on a set of highly replicable energy efficiency and CSI technologies and their viability, which could support demand-side energy efficiency and may apply to major energy-intensive SME sectors, commercial buildings, and electric mobility.

The study had the following objectives:

(i)   understand the market landscape of energy efficiency, CSI, and electric mobility;

(ii) identify attractive lending opportunities for private sector financial institutions for promising energy efficiency and CSI technologies (as recommended products) across various energy-intensive SME industrial sectors, commercial buildings, and electric mobility;

---

[1]   ADB. 2021. DB Raises 2019–2030 Climate Finance Ambition to $100 Billion. News release. 13 October.

(iii)   understand the supplier environment for recommended products with a focus on supply chain assessment and considerations for women-owned or women-led businesses;

(iv)   identify barriers to financing energy efficiency and CSI, with a focus on gender-related barriers to accessing financing for these technologies and probable solutions to address these barriers; and

(v)   identify potential partner private sector financial institutions and energy efficiency and CSI technology vendors seeking future collaboration with ADB.

ABBREVIATIONS

4E	end to end energy efficiency
ADB	Asian Development Bank
BEE	Bureau of Energy Efficiency (Government of India)
CAPEX	capital expenditure
CLCSS	Credit Linked Capital Subsidy Scheme
CO_2	carbon dioxide
COVID-19	coronavirus disease
CSI	climate-smart infrastructure
DFC	Development Finance Corporation
DPR	detailed project report
EESL	Energy Efficiency Services Limited
EFL	Electronica Finance Limited
ESCO	energy service company
ESPC	energy saving performance contract
FAME	Faster Adoption and Manufacturing of (Hybrid and) Electric Vehicles
FCDO	Foreign Common Wealth & Development Office
FEEM	Financing Energy Efficiency at MSMEs
GEF	Global Environment Facility
GHG	greenhouse gas
ICE	internal combustion engine
IFC	International Finance Corporation
IoT	Internet of Things
IREDA	Indian Renewable Energy Development Agency Limited
JICA	Japan International Cooperation Agency
LSP	local service provider

M&V	measurement and verification
MoMSME	Ministry of Micro, Small and Medium Enterprises
MSMEs	micro, small, and medium-sized enterprises
NBFC	nonbanking financial company
NDC	nationally determined contribution
OEM	original equipment manufacturer
PLI	production-linked incentive
PRGFEE	Partial Risk Guarantee Fund for Energy Efficiency
PRSF	partial risk sharing facility
PV	photovoltaic
PwC	PricewaterhouseCoopers Private limited
RBI	Reserve Bank of India
SFB	small finance bank
SIDBI	Small Industries Development Bank of India
SMEs	small and medium-sized enterprises
SPEED	SIDBI – Loan for Purchase of Equipment for Enterprise's Development
TA	technical assistance
TEQUP	Technology Upgradation Scheme for Micro, Small, and Medium Enterprises
TUFS	Technology Upgradation Funding Scheme
UN	United Nations
UNIDO	United Nations Industrial Development Organization
UNNATEE	Unlocking National Energy Efficiency Potential
USAID	United States Agency for International Development

Weights, Measurements, and Conversions

$1.00	=	₹80.00
₹1.00	=	$0.125
1 toe	=	1×10^7 kCal
1 kWh	=	860 kCal
kCal	=	kilocalorie
kWh	=	kilowatt-hour
mtoe	=	million tons of oil equivalent
toe	=	ton of oil equivalent

EXECUTIVE SUMMARY

Opportunities Under Climate Financing

Investments in energy efficiency and climate-smart infrastructure (CSI) can significantly reduce energy costs and greenhouse gas (GHG) emissions. The purpose of this study is to outline viable investment opportunities for private sector financial institutions—both banking and nonbanking financial companies in India across three targeted sectors: (i) energy-intensive small and medium-sized enterprise industrial sectors; (ii) commercial buildings; and (iii) electric mobility for demand-side energy efficiency, as well as other CSI technologies (together referred to as low-carbon technologies).

The conclusions of this study are based on more than 25 consultations with diverse stakeholders including private sector financial institutions, nonbanking financial companies, technology service providers, and energy service companies. They are also based on an evaluation of more than 12 past initiatives in the Indian market focused on promoting large-scale adoption of energy efficiency and CSI technologies across the targeted sectors through various innovative financial instruments.

Survey results indicate that the uptake of these low-carbon technologies has been impacted by various demand- and supply-side challenges. These challenges include limited awareness among the end consumers, the higher up-front cost of energy efficiency and CSI technologies, limited availability of a skilled workforce to adopt or operate these technologies, import dependence and limited reach of technology service providers, and the reluctance of financial institutions to finance these technologies due to various reasons such as perceived performance risks, smaller ticket sizes, higher transaction efforts and costs.

Results reveal that targeted sectors offer significant energy savings and investment opportunities during 2023–2033 and beyond. Commercialized energy efficiency and CSI technologies may offer immense business and financing potential for private sector financial institutions with minimal risks. Partnerships among private players, demand aggregation, and tailored financial products, backed by risk sharing and/or mitigation instruments, will lead to more sustainable and scaled financing solutions.

India is the world's third-largest energy-consuming and carbon-emitting country. Increasing economic development and a growing population—together with the trend toward continued urbanization and industrialization—will further enhance energy demand and therefore increase carbon emissions. This is a critical challenge considering the need for energy security and to reduce and mitigate the carbon emissions impact of energy consumption on the environment.

A focus on energy efficiency and the adoption of CSI technologies in major energy-consuming sectors of the economy can contribute to economic growth while minimizing negative environmental impacts and improving economic efficiency and competitiveness. Mobilizing investment for low-carbon technologies can significantly limit energy intensity and therefore GHG emissions, and may steer India toward a more climate-resilient economy with energy security and sustainable development.

India has made significant progress in improving its energy efficiency and reducing emission intensity by targeting large energy-intensive industries and other sectors of the economy through policy mandates and structured market-based schemes and programs. However, the adoption of energy efficiency and CSI technologies by small and medium-sized enterprises (SMEs) has been limited, and opportunities are yet to be tapped due to the limited availability of tailored financing products suitable for energy efficiency, CSI, and electric mobility (e-mobility). The Reserve Bank of India (RBI) recognizes the need for enhanced participation of domestic financial institutions to support climate-related investments and sustainability financing.

The country partnership strategy for India, 2018–2022 of the Asian Development Bank (ADB) aims to boost economic competitiveness, address climate change, and provide inclusive access to infrastructure. In line with this, ADB—through its Private Sector Operations Department—has elected to support SMEs with the expected impacts by helping to unlock financing opportunities in energy efficiency and CSI while addressing the associated risks, thus enabling the reduction of energy intensity of the Indian economy.

This study focuses on the assessment of viable investment opportunities across various energy-intensive SME industrial sectors, commercial buildings, and e-mobility for energy efficiency and CSI through the engagement of private sector financial institutions and nonbanking financial companies (NBFCs).

Potential for Energy Efficiency and Greenhouse Gas Emission Reduction

Energy Efficiency and Climate-Smart Infrastructure Technologies

The manufacturing industry, commercial buildings, and transport are three major energy-consuming sectors that account for around two-thirds of primary energy demand. As per the national strategic plan (2017–2031) developed by the Government of India Bureau of Energy Efficiency, these three sectors hold more than 75% of India's energy savings potential, which is more than 68 million tons of oil equivalent (mtoe) in a moderate scenario and more than 102 mtoe in an ambitious scenario by 2031.

The investment potential for energy efficiency and CSI deployment in the three sectors is huge, and is estimated to be over $705 billion between 2022 and 2032. Commercial buildings have the largest investment potential at $300 billion, followed by transport at $266 billion, and industries at around $140 billion.

This potential also points to the significant financing need for targeted opportunities in these sectors to leverage financing through private sector financial institutions.

This report identifies eight energy-intensive SME industrial subsectors, along with the commercial buildings and e-mobility sectors, to provide an overview of attractive lending opportunities for private sector financial institutions in India with a set of highly promising energy efficiency and CSI technologies.

Around 60 promising commercialized, semi-commercialized, and state-of-the-art (leading-edge or futuristic) energy efficiency and CSI technologies were short-listed based on defined selection criteria focusing on energy savings potential, investment potential, typical payback, GHG emission reduction potential, market acceptance, and replication potential. Energy savings potential for most technologies ranges from 5% to 30%, with a few technologies having a higher energy efficiency potential of up to 50%. These technologies offer significant potential for energy savings and GHG emission reductions of over 850 million metric tons by 2030.

This compilation of promising technologies is an attempt to offer a guide for financing institutions considering planning or expanding on their energy efficiency, CSI, and e-mobility financing portfolio, as well as for technology providers and energy service companies intending to collaborate with financing institutions and NBFCs.

The commercialized technologies with medium (1–3 years) and long (>3 years) payback periods offer greater potential for financing as these are widely adopted technologies and have vast replication potential. As the credit requirement is usually for smaller loan amounts (up to $125,000) for these solutions, strategic partnerships among financial institutions and technology service providers may support the aggregation of demand and bundling of the loans to make the business more lucrative.

Electric Mobility

The Government of India has a target of around 30% penetration of electric vehicles by 2030 in the total sales of new vehicles. India's electric vehicle adoption will likely vary for different vehicle categories—which will be dominated by two- and three-wheelers—and around 80% of vehicles from these categories will be electric vehicles by 2030. Forecasts also estimate that around 50% of four-wheelers and 30% of buses will also be electric by 2030.

Achieving these targets may result in a cumulative oil savings of around 474 mtoe over the total deployed vehicles' lifetime, which will lead to a carbon emission reduction of around 846 mtoe and monetary savings of more than $185 billion at 2019 prices.

Key Challenges to the Large-Scale Adoption of Energy Efficiency and Climate-Smart Infrastructure Technologies and Electric Mobility

Technology Supply Chain-Level Challenges

This report surveys a supplier environment for the identified products with a focus on supply chain assessment and additional challenges for women-owned or women-led businesses.

Industrial Small and Medium-Sized Enterprise Sectors and Commercial Buildings

Primary consultations with various technology suppliers indicate that one-time up-front payment is the prominent business model for energy efficiency and CSI technologies, and more than 75% of the technology providers operate with this model. The low credibility of SMEs to repay and the risk associated with payment recovery through deferred mechanisms contribute to this trend. Very few technology vendors are practicing leasing with regular payouts based on the operations and leasing business models due to associated business risks.

Some of the prominent challenges in the targeted sectors are

(i)   import dependence;

(ii)   limited reach of energy efficiency and CSI technology providers;

(iii) limited availability of skilled labor for the execution and efficient operation of energy efficiency and CSI technologies; and

(iv) Needed adequate framework for the measurement and verification of actual results (i.e., energy savings and GHG emission reduction achieved) against committed and/or estimated outcomes.

Electric Mobility

E-mobility technologies and the market are both evolving and have several business risks including technology risks and business model risks related to evolving adoption levels, charging infrastructure viability, and secondary markets. A risk-guarantee mechanism backed by the government and/or development banks is needed to accelerate investment through private sector financial institutions.

Some of the prominent challenges in the targeted sectors are:

(i) import dependency on the batteries and components required for electric vehicles;

(ii) lack of an adequate ecosystem of the charging infrastructure;

(iii) limited range of electric vehicles and a higher initial cost;

(iv) unviable charging infrastructure business model (i.e., having a poor return on investment); and

(v) resale risk (the absence of a strong secondary market).

Technology Demand-level Challenges

More than 70% of the consulted technology providers indicated that higher up-front costs (with the resulting high payback periods) and limited awareness regarding energy efficiency and CSI technologies among SMEs limited demand by the end user.

Technology Financing Challenges

This study attempts to recognize the major barriers to financing energy efficiency and CSI across the targeted sectors and gender-related barriers to accessing financing for these technologies in India.

Financial institutions are reluctant to finance energy efficiency and CSI technologies to individual SMEs due to smaller loan sizes and higher transaction efforts and costs. The average ticket size of energy efficiency and CSI loans generally ranges from a few thousands of dollars to $125,000, which is not a lucrative business proposition for financial institutions as handling these small-sized loan portfolios will require more effort and resources resulting in increased transaction costs.

The financing of energy efficiency, CSI, and e-mobility portfolios have different challenges, and these are therefore treated separately throughout this report. The energy efficiency and CSI and e-mobility portfolios and related risk guarantee mechanisms are therefore best treated separately. Some of the other prominent challenges in the targeted sectors are as follows:

Industrial SME Sectors and Commercial Buildings

(i) Preference for balance sheet-based and collateral-backed financing by financial institutions,

(ii) Limited project or asset-based financing,

(iii) Limited knowledge about the energy savings resulting from the various technologies on the part of financial institutions,

(iv)   Higher risk perception of technologies requiring customization that results in higher financing costs, and

(v)   Limited share of private sector financial institutions or NBFCs due to high-cost financing.

Electric Mobility

(i)   Higher up-front costs of electric vehicles compared to their traditional internal combustion engine counterparts,

(ii)   Nonviability of the business model for charging infrastructure (due to lower utilization),

(iii) Financial institutions' limited understanding of e-mobility technology, and

(iv)   Higher interest premiums charged due to perceived inherent risks associated with electric vehicles.

Solutions to Unlock the Potential for Scaling Climate Finance

To catalyze the scaling of climate finance, innovative solutions are essential. The following strategies present effective avenues for unlocking potential in this critical sector. These include portfolio-based risk guarantee mechanisms, long-term lines of credit from international development associations, and strategic partnerships among private players for tailored financial products. Each approach aims to mitigate risks, lower financing costs, and foster sustainable market mechanisms, thereby accelerating the adoption of energy efficiency and CSI technologies.

(i)   **Portfolio-based risk guarantee mechanisms,** where risk cover is offered to financial institutions and NBFCs over their entire portfolio of projects, have some distinct advantages. These solutions offer financial institutions the flexibility to provide varying degrees of coverage based on their risk assessment on individual projects. This helps to optimize the guarantee fee component by providing need-based coverage. Risk guarantee mechanisms specific to business models—like the energy service company model for energy efficiency—are already in place. Risk guarantee mechanisms that are agnostic to business models will help to expand coverage across the entire spectrum of energy efficiency, CSI, and e-mobility projects where there is a legitimate risk perception at financial institutions. Simplicity and user-friendly processes—coupled with moderate guarantee fees—are critical to their success.

(ii)   **Long-term portfolio-based lines of credit offerings from international development associations to NBFCs and financial institutions** can be relevant, especially in the context of the marginally higher cost of finance offered by NBFCs. NBFCs can pass on the benefits of lower interest rates to stakeholders in the financing ecosystem, improving the viability and/or attractiveness of the projects and potentially improving the demand. NBFCs should ideally retain the flexibility to decide on interest rates based on the specific risk profiles of individual loan cases. NBFCs are sometimes better placed for energy efficiency and CSI financing based on their portfolio, exposure to the sector dynamics, their ability to evaluate the energy efficiency or CSI projects, etc.

(iii) **Partnerships among private players, demand aggregation, and tailored financial product offerings backed by a risk sharing or mitigation instrument** will lead to a sustainable market mechanism. Experiences from previous schemes, programs, projects, or studies implemented by various Indian national and international agencies, and consultations with stakeholders, indicate a need to develop tailored financial products backed by a public finance and risk mitigation mechanism to support large-scale adoption of identified products in targeted sectors. A collaborative approach by private sector financial institutions (commonly referred to as FIs in the Indian context) through partnerships with suitable technology suppliers can extend support to the end consumer on both ends. It will support the demand aggregation for technologies as well as loans, which will create a sustainable market mechanism to drive energy efficiency and CSI technology business for a longer period.

This study attempts to identify some of the probable solutions to address the barriers to financing energy efficiency and CSI technologies in targeted sectors.

The report also attempts to analyze strengths, weaknesses, opportunities, and threats (SWOT) for financing energy efficiency and CSI in targeted sectors through SWOT analysis. Energy efficiency and e-mobility are driven by policy, and the Government of India has been supporting the development of the policy ecosystem for promoting a conducive environment for developing energy efficiency and CSI technologies. The government is also fostering the adoption of these technologies through regulatory mandates for the applicable sectors. To support faster implementation and adoption by each sector, the government provides financial incentives to the front-runners. Through this holistic framework, the government is creating an ecosystem to support sustainability.

RBI has also been supporting clean energy adoption through initiatives such as "priority sector lending." To assess the progress of the regulated entities in managing climate risk, RBI published a discussion paper to understand the risks associated with clean energy and sustainability financing with regulated entities.

RBI and different ministries are planning to widen priority sector lending to develop a strong platform to foster the financing of energy efficiency and e-mobility. Driven by significant opportunities and backed by a conducive environment, private financing can play a pivotal role in redefining the new age of energy efficiency and e-mobility with new financing solutions.

1 INTRODUCTION

India is home to more than 1.38 billion people (around 17.8% of the global population), is one of the world's fastest-growing economies, and is the world's third-largest energy-consuming country. The per capita energy use and emissions of India are less than half of the world average; however, improved affordability and access to energy, continued urbanization, and industrialization will increase energy demand.

The efficient use of energy and restricting energy wastage is essential to meet future energy demand and pursue sustainable development. The Government of India Bureau of Energy Efficiency (BEE) has developed a national strategic plan toward developing an energy-efficient nation (2017–2031): *Unlocking National Energy Efficiency Potential* (UNNATEE).[1]

The report forecasted future energy demand under different scenarios for various sectors of the economy until 2031 as a principal step toward the estimation of energy efficiency potential (Table 1).

Table 1: Projected Energy Consumption of High-Energy Sectors by 2031

Sectors of Economy	Energy Consumption 2031 (mtoe)		
	Least Effort Scenario	Moderate Effort Scenario	Ambitious Effort Scenario
Commercial	29.5	24.5	23.1
Industrial	443.4	396.0	371.2
Transport	232.9	217.2	209.1
Total	**705.8**	**637.7**	603.4

mtoe = million tons of oil equivalent.
Source: Government of India, Bureau of Energy Efficiency. 2019. *Unlocking National Energy Efficiency Potential (UNNATEE): Strategy Plan Towards Developing an Energy Efficient Nation (2017–2031)*. New Delhi.

India has energy savings potential in the following sectors: (i) commercial (including energy efficiency in buildings and climate-smart infrastructure [CSI] technologies, energy conservation building code compliant buildings); (ii) industrial (including small and medium-sized enterprises [SMEs], large industries with a potential for energy efficiency, smart infrastructure technologies such as Internet of Things [IoT], Industry 4.0, automation, machine learning, artificial intelligence, etc.); and (iii) transport (fuel efficiency standards, improved penetration of clean energy fuel vehicles). This potential is estimated to be 68.2 million tons of oil equivalent (mtoe) with a "moderate" implementation of energy efficiency programs, and an estimate of 102.5 mtoe with an "ambitious" implementation

---

[1]   Government of India, Bureau of Energy Efficiency. 2019. *Unlocking National Energy Efficiency Potential (UNNATEE): Strategy Plan Towards Developing an Energy Efficient Nation (2017–2031)*. New Delhi.

of energy efficiency programs. This would result in a 15% reduction in energy demand by 2031 compared to the "business-as-usual" approach. To meet this target, the estimated investment for energy efficiency interventions will amount to ~$117 billion for the ambitious scenario, with the highest energy savings investment potential in the industrial sector (Table 2).

Table 2: Energy Savings and Investment Potential for Sectors of Economy (until 2031)

Sectors of Economy	Energy Savings Potential 2031 (mtoe)		Energy Efficiency Investment Potential by 2031 ($ billion)	
	Moderate Scenario	Ambitious Scenario	Moderate Scenario	Ambitious Scenario
Commercial	4.9	6.4	10	13
Industrial	47.5	72.3	38	58
Transport	15.8	23.8	28	46
Total	68.2	102.5	76	117

mtoe = million tons of oil equivalent.
Source: Government of India, Bureau of Energy Efficiency. 2019. _Unlocking National Energy Efficiency Potential (UNNATEE): Strategy Plan Towards Developing an Energy Efficient Nation (2017–2031)_. New Delhi.

The energy sector is one of the major contributors to greenhouse gas (GHG) emissions and accounts for about 75.6% of total GHG emissions.[2] India is committed to addressing the challenge of climate change associated with economic growth and increased energy demand and has progressively adopted cleaner energy in different sectors to reduce GHG emissions. The rising quantum of energy signifies the potential for GHG emissions reductions in various sectors (Table 3).

Table 3: Greenhouse Gas Emission Reduction Potential for Study Sectors

Sectors of Economy	GHG Emission Reduction Potential by 2030 (mtCo$_2$e)	
	Moderate Scenario	Ambitious Scenario
Commercial	34	44
Industrial	185	238
Transport	97	141
Total	316	423

GHG = greenhouse gas, mtCO$_2$e = million tons of carbon dioxide equivalent.
Note: Energy efficiency: Equipment and processes that consume lower energy than conventional operations.
Source: Government of India, Bureau of Energy Efficiency. 2019. _Unlocking National Energy Efficiency Potential (UNNATEE): Strategy Plan Towards Developing an Energy Efficient Nation (2017–2031)_. New Delhi.

Accelerating the adoption of energy efficiency, the deployment of CSI technologies, and demand-side electrification with enhanced integration of renewable energy sources on the supply side will steer India toward a low-carbon economy.

---

[2] World Resources Institute. 2020. 4 Charts Explain Greenhouse Gas Emissions by Countries and Sectors.

Need for the Study

Major energy-intensive sectors of the economy, such as industries, commercial buildings, and transport, account for over two-thirds of national primary energy consumption (553 mtoe) and offer significant energy savings and GHG emissions reduction potential.[3]

The substantial scaling up of investments in energy efficiency,[4] CSI in industries and commercial buildings (especially in small and medium-sized establishments), and the electrification of vehicle fleets would require new and substantial financial resources and support.[5]

Despite an immense investment potential in the energy efficiency and CSI market, business is taking off in a limited way due to various challenges across the supply chain, from financial institutions and technology suppliers to end users. There have been challenges in making energy efficiency and CSI a convincing business case, and this has impacted the capital flow to the market. These challenges are a combination of knowledge, technical, and financial barriers. The energy efficiency and CSI market still calls for a well-planned strategy and effective instruments to develop a sustainable market mechanism.

Public programs and participation from private players are needed to address these challenges and realize the full potential of the market. Private sector financial institutions would play a critical role in mainstreaming financing for energy efficiency and CSI technologies with their regular business activities.

Investments in energy efficiency, CSI, and electric mobility (e-mobility) contribute directly to climate change mitigation, which is of national priority. India submitted its nationally determined contributions (NDCs) target to the United Nations Framework Convention on Climate Change intending to reduce the emissions intensity of its gross domestic product (GDP). India also voluntarily committed to being a carbon-neutral economy by 2070.[6]

The Reserve Bank of India (RBI) published a discussion paper that highlights various risks for financial institutions and threats to local and global financial stability due to climate change with an intent to prepare a strategy based on global best practices for mitigating the adverse impacts of climate change. RBI drafted the paper to address the challenges and develop long-term risk mitigation plans to support and foster the uptake of climate financing, including the financing of energy efficiency and CSI.[7]

The discussion paper also highlighted that financial institutions should manage the risks and opportunities that may arise from climate change and environmental degradation.

In this evolving framework for promoting private sector lending toward energy efficiency, CSI, and e-mobility—and given the substantial need for financial sector investment—it is important to identify the barriers faced by financial institutions in filling this financing need. This report describes the needs of financial institutions and the measures required to allow them to provide specialized financial products to mainstream access to energy efficiency and CSI—including in the building and mobility sectors—to achieve India's emissions reduction goals.

---

[3] Government of India, Ministry of Statistics and Programme Implementation. 2021. *Energy Statistics India 2021* (accessed 7 December 2023).

[4] Energy efficiency: Equipment and processes that consume lower energy than conventional operations.

[5] CSI includes the use of sophisticated sensors, modern IoT, digital integration, process automation, use of artificial intelligence and machine learning through programming, process optimization of operations, and energy conservation.

[6] *BBC News India*. 2021. COP26: India PM Narendra Modi Pledges Net Zero by 2070. 2 November.

[7] Reserve Bank of India. n.d. Discussion Paper on Climate Risk and Sustainable Finance.

The Targeted Sectors

Industrial Sector (Small and Medium-Sized Enterprises)

The manufacturing industry is the largest consumer of energy (328 mtoe) in terms of primary energy consumption in India (footnote 1). Larger corporates and large industries have better access to finance and the technical strengths to navigate this transition. SMEs in India (units having investments in plant and machinery or equipment of not more than $6.25 million and an annual turnover of not more than $31.25 million) will require ongoing guidance and innovative financing solutions to adopt clean energy technology and solutions.

The SME sector contributes around 25% of energy consumption and is a critical growth driver of the Indian economy.[8] This sector contributes to nearly 30% of GDP and holds significant potential to steer India toward a low-carbon economy. SMEs in India can be segregated into over 17 of the most energy-intensive industries such as foundries, textiles, ceramics, refractories, glass, dairy, buildings, e-mobility, etc. Because they use obsolete technologies and poor operating practices, SMEs offer significant potential for energy savings through energy efficiency and CSI adoptions. In addition to reduced energy consumption, local pollutants and GHG emissions are also eliminated by energy efficiency and CSI to achieve regulatory requirements and government targets. However, SMEs have limited technical capabilities to implement energy efficiency and CSI technologies, and limited capacities to access finance due to the lower strength of balance sheets and a lack of collateral.

Affordability and access to finance for energy efficiency technologies in SMEs have been limited in enabling the large-scale deployment of energy efficiency and CSI technologies. SMEs (in industrial manufacturing) in India have been traditionally led and dominated by male entrepreneurs. Based on the emergence of new services and technology-oriented roles (new age technologies, Internet of Things IoT, robotics, automation, Industry 4.0, blockchain, etc.), the share of women in the industrial sector has witnessed growth.

Commercial Buildings

The commercial building sector (mainly comprising hotels, shopping malls, commercial buildings, corporate offices, technology parks, etc.) has seen a significant increase in the consumption of electricity. This consumption is expected to increase due to an increase in building floor space propelled by upcoming economic reforms, growth in various sectors, an improved standard of living, and other factors. India is improving the energy efficiency of buildings through mandatory building energy codes and voluntary rating schemes, as well as through policies and programs to improve the efficiency of appliances. Compared to the manufacturing sector—which is a male-dominated sector—the commercial building sector has a higher presence of women across the different business segments (designing, conducting operations, coding, and developing standards). One of the largest certifying and energy efficiency building authorities—Green Business Certification Inc. (GBCI) India—is led by women and plays a crucial role in the entire value chain of this sector.

Electric Mobility

E-mobility refers to the cleaner fuel-driven road transport network ecosystem. It includes electric vehicles, charging stations, battery-swapping facilities, service providers, etc. The e-mobility market is still in a nascent stage in India. There have been developments concerning the introduction of new regulatory policies, the flow of funds and

---

8   Government of India, Bureau of Energy Efficiency. 2019. *Unlocking National Energy Efficiency Potential (UNNATEE). Strategy Plan Towards Developing an Energy Efficient Nation (2017–2031)*, and Government of India, Ministry of Statistics and Programme Implementation. 2018. *Energy Statistics 2018*. New Delhi.

investments in the sector, an increase in the number of start-ups, etc. This segment is dominated by start-ups and SME players and possesses a higher potential for GHG emission reduction through energy transition.

To decarbonize the transport sector, India is among a handful of countries that have pledged to the global "EV30@30" initiative.[9] To support India's commitment to tackle climate change, the central and state governments have been proactively announcing several policy interventions and incentives to support the whole electric vehicle ecosystem.

Compared to the manufacturing sector—which is male dominated—most e-mobility start-ups have a higher contribution of women at the different management levels providing impetus for this new energy transition drive. Evolving e-mobility and last-mile delivery are also empowering Indian women toward self-reliance through new job creation. This evolving sector of the Indian economy is supporting the new era of gender equality and promoting the share of women entrepreneurs and businesses.

The Framework Adopted During the Study and Summary of the Sections

An open, adaptive, and consultative framework with a methodology combining secondary research and primary consultations was adopted for the study. The broader objective of the study was to map the needs and requirements to bridge the challenges and gaps that are prevalent in the energy efficiency and CSI ecosystem. The focus of the study was to map the financial interventions and extent of the financing required to foster the uptake of the energy efficiency and CSI financing to support India to meet its NDC goals and long-term decarbonization.

The approach and methodology adopted during the study, including the step-by-step procedures, are provided in Appendix 1 and Appendix 2.

The study outlined a comprehensive review of market benchmarking for SME investment in energy efficiency and CSI technologies and is organized in the following chapters of this report:

Chapter 2: Market Landscape of Energy Efficiency, Climate-Smart Infrastructure, and E-mobility. This chapter elaborates on the energy consumption and energy savings potential for the different sectors, i.e., SMEs in the industry, building, and e-mobility sectors.

Chapter 3: Energy-Intensive Sectors and Technologies. To tailor energy efficiency products, major energy-intensive sectors and technologies have been mapped under this section. These short-listed key technologies cater to the larger part of energy consumption (Pareto principle). Technologies have been further categorized based on replication potential, cost, and commercialization aspects.

Chapter 4: Supply Chain for Energy Efficiency, Climate-Smart Infrastructure, and E-mobility Technologies. The study mapped the supply chain and how different players of the supply chain work together. The chapter also presents the major challenges and barriers faced by prominent partners and stakeholders and details key linkages of the different partners working in the ecosystem.

Chapter 5: Analyzing the Schemes and Policies Landscape. Schemes and programs for energy efficiency, CSI, and e-mobility are presented. The study mapped key learning and takeaways, and the success and penetration level of the different programmatic interventions.

---

[9] NITI Aayog and Rocky Mountain Institute. 2019. India's Electric Mobility Transformation.

Chapter 6: Strengths, Weaknesses, Opportunities, and Threats Analysis and Policy Recommendations. This Chapter details strengths, weaknesses, opportunities, and threats (SWOT) for the sectors under study and outlines prospects in these sectors that can be strengthened through a policy and regulatory framework. The study team also carried out a SWOT analysis for the ecosystem to map the possible long-term strategic interventions planned under energy efficiency, CSI, and e-mobility.

Chapter 7: Barriers and Opportunities in Financing Energy Efficiency, Climate-Smart Infrastructure, and E-mobility. This chapter details the challenges and barriers faced by private sector financial institutions and nonbanking financial companies (NBFCs). The study provides detailed interventions and solutions that will foster private sector financing for energy efficiency, CSI, and e-mobility.

2 MARKET LANDSCAPE OF ENERGY EFFICIENCY, CLIMATE-SMART INFRASTRUCTURE, AND E-MOBILITY

This chapter presents the overall market landscape and investment potential for the sectors covered (i.e., industries, buildings, and transport) under the study.[10] The energy savings potential and emission reduction from these energy conservation measures are also analyzed.

Understanding the Energy Efficiency and Climate-Smart Infrastructure Energy Savings and Investment Potential

The industrial segment contributes to the bulk of energy consumption in India. Among this share, the micro, small, and medium-sized enterprise (MSME) sector contributes around 25% of the overall industrial energy consumption, estimated at ~82 mtoe. Commercial buildings have an energy consumption of 9 mtoe. Nationally, there is immense potential to be realized from the large-scale implementation of energy efficiency interventions in various demand sectors.

BEE has developed a national strategy plan Unlocking National Energy Efficiency Potential (UNNATEE).[11] India's energy savings potential is estimated to be 86.9 mtoe in the case of a "moderate" implementation of energy efficiency programs, while the estimate is 129 mtoe using "ambitious" programs by 2031, resulting in a 15% reduction in energy demand compared to the baseline year of 2017 (Table 4).

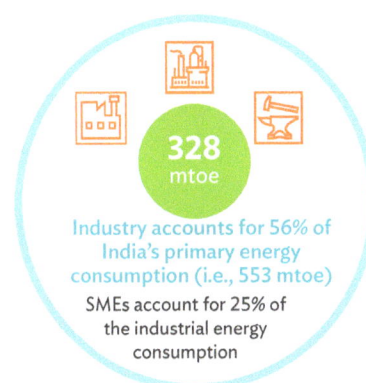

328 mtoe

Industry accounts for 56% of India's primary energy consumption (i.e., 553 mtoe)

SMEs account for 25% of the industrial energy consumption

Table 4: Sector Energy Efficiency Potential until 2031

Sector	Energy Efficiency Potential until 2031 (mtoe)	
	Moderate Scenario	Ambitious Scenario
Industrial (including SMEs)	47.5	72.3
Commercial Buildings	4.9	6.4

mtoe = million tons of oil equivalent, SMEs = small and medium-sized enterprises.
Source: Government of India, Bureau of Energy Efficiency. *Unlocking Energy Efficiency Potential (UNNATEE). Strategy Plan Toward Developing an Energy Efficient Nation (2017-2031).*

---

[10] Considering the similarity and variabilities involved across different sectors, i.e., industries, buildings, and transport (e-mobility), industries and buildings have been placed together for ease of analysis and e-mobility is presented as a separate subsection throughout this report.
[11] Data mentioned in this chapter (except for the potential of CSI) have been taken from the UNNATEE report published by the Bureau of Energy Efficiency.

To cater to the estimated energy efficiency potential per the national strategy plan, investment for **energy efficiency amounts to $140 billion over 14 years**. The industrial sector—including SMEs—will contribute to around 50%–60% of total energy savings potential and has the **energy efficiency investment potential of $40 billion–$60 billion by 2031**.

In addition to energy efficiency, **CSI** possesses enormous investment potential estimated at **$3 trillion during 2018–2030** (International Finance Corporation [IFC] study on Smart Infrastructure in India).[12] Green buildings will contribute around 50% of this investment potential by 2030. SMEs such as commercial buildings, shopping complexes, hotels, etc. will require an investment potential of ~$300 billion by 2031.

UNNATEE projects a GHG emission reduction potential of **185 metric tons of carbon dioxide in the industrial sector. Energy efficiency and CSI deployment in the buildings sector** will potentially reduce GHG emissions by **34 metric tons of carbon dioxide by 2030**.

There is huge potential for energy savings. However, different scales of industries and buildings have different priorities and expertise for the execution of energy efficiency and climate strategies. Large industries and corporations have access to adequate resources, strong technical teams, and are well-equipped to leverage different financing options to support energy efficiency interventions compared to the SME sector where technical capabilities and capacities to access finance are limited. The immense quantum of energy consumed by the SME sector offers potential for energy savings through technology upgradation, energy efficiency, CSI retrofits in the production processes, and the adoption of best-in-class technologies.

Energy efficiency is generally perceived as a secondary aspect when compared to the core business activity or is only considered when it directly links to an increase in production or output in the SME sector. This perception is also generated by a lack of awareness about energy efficiency especially in the SME sector.

Fuel prices have increased steeply. At the same time, long-term initiatives have been planned by the Government of India such as net zero emissions by 2070, the promotion of the Energy Conservation Building Code, promoting ISO 50001, IoT, Industry 4.0 (including automation, process optimization, virtual audits, real-time monitoring and controls), energy management systems, etc. The coronavirus disease (COVID-19) pandemic also brought to light inherent issues related to skilled labor and created an inclination toward digitization and automation through CSI and Industry 4.0 technologies.

All these trends have cumulatively resulted in a gradual, but definite, attitudinal shift in SMEs toward adopting modern energy efficiency and CSI technologies. Adoption of energy efficiency and CSI technologies will empower SMEs to reduce the cost of production and become more competitive.

To support this transformation, some key players in the ecosystem will play a pivotal role. It is imperative to understand key subsectors and the associated supply chain. During the detailed analysis, subsectors having the highest potential for energy savings were mapped, which will help in drafting focused solutions.

---

[12]   International Finance Corporation. 2017. IFC Analysis Points to $3.4 trillion in Climate-Smart Investment Opportunities in South Asia. Press Release. 29 November.

Understanding the E-mobility Market Opportunity in India

To decarbonize the transport sector, India is among a handful of countries that have pledged to the global "EV30@30" initiative. As part of this initiative, the target is to have at least a 30% share of electric vehicles among the total new vehicle sales (footnote 1). To support India's commitment to tackle climate change, the central and state governments have been proactively announcing several policy interventions and incentives to support the whole electric vehicle ecosystem ranging from manufacturing vehicles, batteries, and battery packs to developing a robust charging infrastructure.

58.7 mtoe

Transport accounts for ~9.5% of India's primary energy consumption
Road transport accounts for 75% of energy consumption

To create an entire value chain around e-mobility in India, significant investments will be required at each step. This presents massive investment opportunities for every key stakeholder.

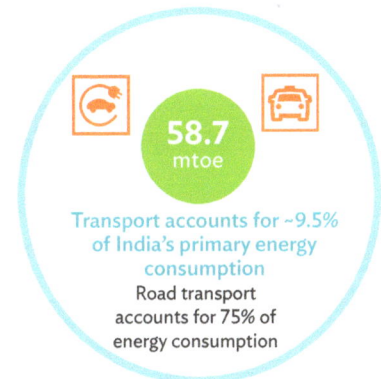

Investment Opportunities for Original Equipment Manufacturers (Vehicle Manufacturers)

Two-wheeler electric vehicles are expected to be the primary driver of electric vehicle sales in the country, with an annual production cost of $1 billion expected in fiscal year (FY) 2021.[13] This is expected to increase to $19 billion by FY2030.[14] To meet the target of 80% electric vehicle sales by 2030, **the cumulative cost is expected to be more than $91 billion during 2021–2030**.

Total production costs of four-wheeler electric vehicles are expected to be around $20 billion by FY2030 to meet the tentative target of around 30% new electric vehicle sales. The total cumulative production cost is expected to be around $74 billion by 2030.

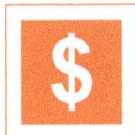

$ This presents total investment opportunities of around **$177 billion from FY2021 to FY2030** which includes fixed-cost investments such as those required to scale up assembly lines and product capacity to meet the respective targets.[15]

Investment Opportunity for Battery Manufacturing

As of March 2022, close to 80% of lithium-ion batteries for electric vehicles running in the country were produced locally.[16] The demand for battery manufacturing is driven by the sale of new electric vehicles and the demand for the replacement of batteries in existing electric vehicles.

Investment Opportunity for Developing Charging Infrastructure

Developing a robust charging infrastructure network is critical to the success of an electric vehicle ecosystem. Public charging infrastructure is not solely proportional to the number of electric vehicles sold; it is critically dependent on the vehicle categories and their electric vehicle charging requirements. In a study on the charging

---

[13] Data points under this section are taken from Government of India, NITI Aayog and Deutsche Gesellschaft für Internationale Zusammenarbeit. 2021. *Status Quo Analysis of Various Segments of Electric Mobility and Low Carbon Passenger Road Transport in India*. New Delhi.

[14] The fiscal year of the Government of India ends on 31 March.

[15] Centre for Energy Finance. Financing India's Transition to Electric Vehicles.

[16] Press briefing, Road Transports and Highways Minister Nitin Gadkari. 19 March 2022.

infrastructure of Europe—which has a far more developed electric vehicle ecosystem—only ~20% of the two-wheelers, ~50% of the three-wheelers, ~20% of the personal four-wheeler vehicles, and ~50% of the commercial four-wheeler electric vehicles required public charging facilities.[17]

Based on the projected vehicle sales in India until 2030, it is expected that cumulative investments of around **$3 billion** will be required to build a well-connected public charging network, especially across all urban areas and highways within India.[18]

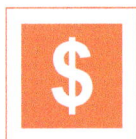

The clean energy investment potential has been identified for these three key sectors. Investment potential is **$50 billion** for industry, **$300 billion** for commercial buildings, and **$266 billion** for road transport to support long-term energy efficiency and energy CSI requirements during 2023–2033. **These three sectors possess an overall investment potential of over $615 billion (including the energy efficiency and CSI potential for the SME industrial sector, commercial buildings, and e-mobility).**

---

[17] Government of India, NITI Aayog and Deutsche Gesellschaft für Internationale Zusammenarbeit. 2021. *Status Quo Analysis of Various Segments of Electric Mobility and Low Carbon Passenger Road Transport in India*. New Delhi.

[18] Based on a PwC estimation for the sector by key experts.

3 ENERGY-INTENSIVE SECTORS AND TECHNOLOGIES

This section maps and analyzes energy-intensive SME sectors to identify energy efficiency technology and CSI solutions. This analysis leads to suggesting tailored solutions and recommendations for an energy efficiency, CSI, and e-mobility financing strategy to be developed for the SME sector.

Mapping and ranking of the various sectors based on aggregate energy consumption, energy cost share, and number of SME units in the sector are presented in this chapter, as well as energy efficiency, CSI, and e-mobility technologies that have high replication potential and a need for—and amenability to—third-party financing (see section on Mapping Energy Efficiency Technologies for Energy-Intensive Small and Medium-Sized Enterprises).

These sectors and technologies can serve as focus areas for developing tailored financial products that help in promoting long-term sustainable goals and contribute to GHG emission reductions in line with India's NDC commitments.[19] Gaining an appreciation of the key market sectors and technologies, along with the supply chain dynamics, is vital.

Mapping Energy-Intensive Sectors (Small and Medium-Sized Enterprises, Commercial Buildings, and E-mobility)

The SME sector in India comprises organized (registered units) and a sizable unorganized segment. Out of 60 million enterprises, nearly 20% are manufacturing industries and close to 80% of enterprises come under service sectors.[20]

There is considerable diversity among the industrial units in the manufacturing sector. SMEs in India are segregated into a handful of energy-intensive industrial sectors such as bricks, foundries, forging, textiles, ceramics, refractories, glass, dairy, etc. Several industrial sectors stand out in terms of their energy intensity. Energy costs form a significant share of the manufacturing cost at these SME sectors, with the share of energy cost, accounting sometimes for up to 30% of the total production costs (including raw material cost).

In addition to the industrial manufacturing (SME sectors), buildings and transport also stand out in terms of their energy intensity, market size, and future growth and investment potential.

---

[19] India's NDCs comprise eight goals. Three of these have quantitative targets up to 2030: cumulative electric power installed capacity from nonfossil sources to reach 40%; emissions intensity of GDP to reduce by 33%–35% compared to 2005 levels; and the creation of an additional carbon sink of 2.5 billion–3 billion tons of carbon dioxide equivalent (tCO2e) through additional forest and tree cover.

[20] Government of India, Ministry of Micro, Small and Medium Enterprises. 2022. MoMSME *Annual Report 2020-2021*.

Figure 1: High Energy-Consuming Subsectors

Textile	Steel Re-rolling	Ceramics and Refractory	Foundry	Chemical	Pharma	Plastics
Food	Engineering	Glass	Forging	Paper	Auto	Brass
		Hand tool	Rubber	Sponge Iron		

Source: Government of India, Bureau of Energy Efficiency.

E-mobility is one of the subsegments of the transport sector, which comprises electric vehicles, batteries, and charging infrastructure, and includes several SME players. The sector has exponential growth potential coupled with a high potential for reducing GHG emissions through the energy transition. The energy transition from internal combustion engine (ICE) vehicles to electric vehicles will change the entire ecosystem of the road transport sector and will help in supporting long-term decarbonization goals. Various subcategories in e-mobility include electric vehicles and charging infrastructure, maintenance, and value-added service providers.

Commercial buildings is a subsector that has a significantly high energy intensity trend in the building sector. This sector has contributed to a significant increase in the consumption of electricity. This consumption is expected to increase multifold in the coming years due to an increase in building floor space propelled by upcoming economic reforms, growth in various sectors, improved standard of living, and other factors. This sector will attract policy focus and investments toward energy efficiency and decarbonization. The subcategorization of commercial buildings includes commercial complexes, offices, shopping malls, and hotels.

Identifying Sectors with the Most Energy Savings Potential

Sectors with energy efficiency potential have been ranked by identifying criteria such as absolute energy consumption, average energy intensity, GHG reduction potential, etc.:

| Energy Consumption (toe) – A | Energy Intensity as % of Production Cost - B | Average Energy Efficiency Potential (%) – C | Sector Level Absolute GHG Emissions – D |

The starting point for identifying values against each criterion is a comprehensive scan of previous programmatic interventions. The data gathered through secondary research was validated through stakeholder consultations. Table 5 summarizes the ranking and prioritization of SME manufacturing sectors based on distinct values against each criterion (Appendix 1).

Table 5: Short-Listed Energy-Intensive Small and Medium-Sized Enterprise Sectors

Rank	Sector	Energy Consumption (toe)	Energy Intensity as % of Prod. Cost (%)	Energy Efficiency Potential (%)	Calculated Weights[a]
1	Textile	5,590,040	20–35	8–12	0.75
2	Steel Re-rolling – Total	1,742,352	40–45	10–15	0.72
3	Foundry	1,292,320	40–45	10–15	0.69
4	Forgings	226,236	35–45	10–15	0.59
5	Ceramics and Refractory	1,655,348	25–35	8–10	0.44
6	Paper	137,971	20–25	10–15	0.44
7	Glassware	385,282	25–30	8–10	0.32
8	Brass	117,404	15–20	10–12	0.32

prod = production, toe = tons of oil equivalent.

[a] Calculated weights form the basis for ranks assigned. Refer to Appendix 1 for calculation parameters.

Source: Authors, derived from the SME reports for the different sectors and BEE energy audits report.

Using this prioritization matrix, the top eight energy-intensive SME manufacturing sectors are distilled out. Along with these, the two most pertinent sectors for clean energy financing—buildings and e-mobility—have been used to identify the most promising technologies for financing.

An inclusive approach was adopted, and attempts were made to include some of the most promising technologies irrespective of the sectors in which these are applied.

Mapping Energy Efficiency Technologies for Energy-Intensive Small and Medium-Sized Enterprises

Energy efficiency technologies were mapped by sector based on various criteria such as GHG reduction potential, replication potential, commercial aspects, financial feasibility, etc. The broader objective was the identification of key technologies that have high financing and/or investment potential. This will help in developing the solutions with a focus on key technologies (energy efficiency and CSI) that have a higher contribution in developing sustainable solutions.

Identifying the Most Promising Energy Efficiency and CSI Technologies

The study mapped the most promising energy efficiency and CSI technologies relevant to the energy-intensive MSME sector (see "Mapping Energy-Intensive Sectors" section) using secondary research from multiple resources and the following approach:

Figure 2: Approach for Identifying Most Promising Energy Efficiency and CSI Technologies

Mapping of **subsectors** for energy-intensive sectors → Mapping of **processes/technologies** at sector and subsector levels → Mapping and ranking of energy-efficiency **technologies** relevant to different energy-intensive sectors

Source: Author Analysis.

The study short-listed the top 50–60 most relevant energy efficiency technologies using key qualitative and quantitative criteria. The broader objective of the short-listing exercise was to map key potential technologies that can be used to develop long-term sustainable financing solutions. These criteria include measures of impact in terms of energy conservation, investment potential, and return on investments on the one hand, and measures of scalability like market acceptance and replication potential on the other.

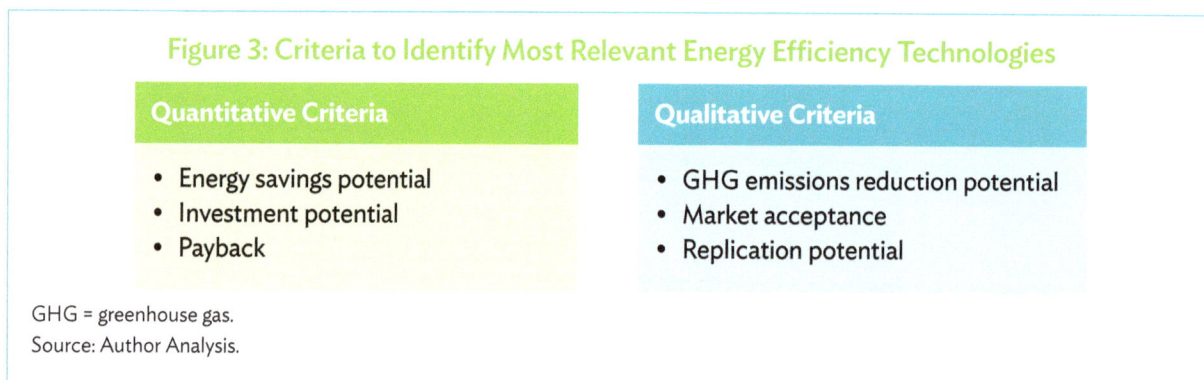

Figure 3: Criteria to Identify Most Relevant Energy Efficiency Technologies

Quantitative Criteria	Qualitative Criteria
• Energy savings potential • Investment potential • Payback	• GHG emissions reduction potential • Market acceptance • Replication potential

GHG = greenhouse gas.
Source: Author Analysis.

This report separated technologies into three major categories (commercialized, semi-commercialized, and state of the art) based on their maturity and availability.

Technologies that are available as off-the-shelf products, require no energy study at the unit level for feasibility assessment, and with enough case studies in the public domain to define the proven energy savings potential, are categorized as **commercial** technologies.

Technologies that require customizations at the unit level, require energy study and baseline assessment before implementation, and have a lower number of proven case studies available are categorized as **semi-commercial**.

Some technologies are relatively new and do not have enough implementation in SMEs, the implementation of technologies requires significant investment but result in significant energy savings. Such technologies are categorized as **state of the art**.

Figure 4 shows the methodology used for the ranking of key energy efficiency technologies.

Based on the parameters in Figure 4, the study ranked the technologies, and the ranking results and methodology were discussed during stakeholder consultations with technology providers and original equipment manufacturers (OEMs). The detailed methodology adopted for short-listing the technology is in Appendix 2. Table 6 summarizes the short-listed technologies based on the rankings from Figure 4.

Figure 4: Methodology Used for Ranking Key Technologies

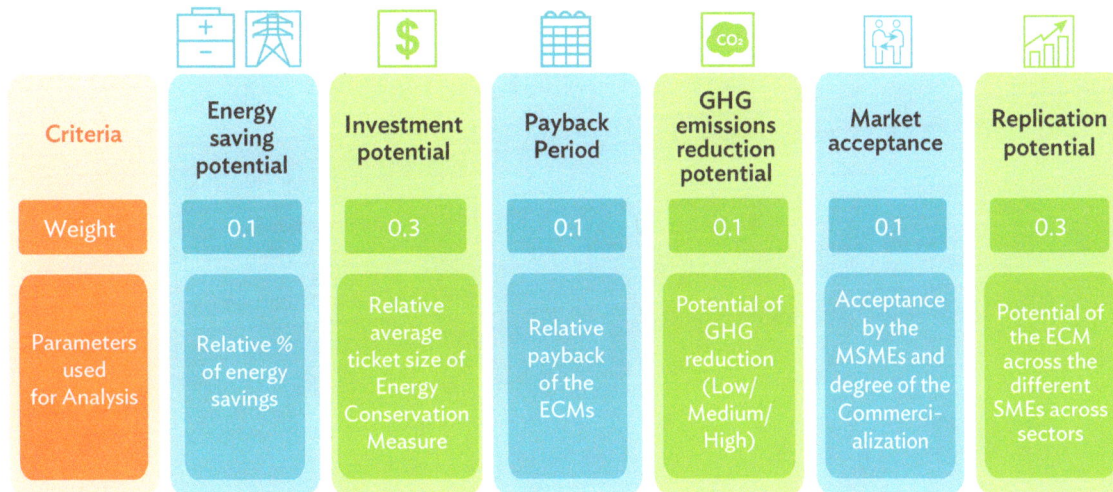

Criteria	Energy saving potential	Investment potential	Payback Period	GHG emissions reduction potential	Market acceptance	Replication potential
Weight	0.1	0.3	0.1	0.1	0.1	0.3
Parameters used for Analysis	Relative % of energy savings	Relative average ticket size of Energy Conservation Measure	Relative payback of the ECMs	Potential of GHG reduction (Low/Medium/High)	Acceptance by the MSMEs and degree of the Commercialization	Potential of the ECM across the different SMEs across sectors

ECM = energy conservation measure; GHG = greenhouse gas; MSMEs = micro, small, and medium-sized enterprises; SMEs = small and medium-sized enterprises.

Source: Authors.

Table 6: Summary of Technologies Based on Short-Listing Criteria

Overall Rank	Technology	Most Applicable Sector	Energy Savings Potential (%)	Ticket size (₹100,000)	Replication Potential (%)	Payback Period (years)	Market Acceptance	GHG Emission Reduction Potential
Industrial Energy Efficiency Technologies								
1.	Induction billet heater for metal heating	Forging	50–75	20–50	High	2–3	Commercialized	High
2.	IGBT induction melting furnace	Foundry	5–15	50–200	High	2–3	Commercialized	High
3.	Centralized space cooling and ventilation	Multiple	10–30	20–100	High	3–5	Commercialized	Medium
4.	Box type billet heating furnaces	Steel and allied sectors	15–35	1–5	High	2–3	Commercialized	High
5.	LED lights	Multiple	40–50	0–1	High	1–2	Commercialized	Medium
6.	EE blowers and fans	Multiple	20–50	3–7	High	3–5	Commercialized	Low
7.	Gas engine with integrated vapor absorption machine/hot water generator	Multiple	20–40	100–500	Low	3–5	Commercialized	Medium
8.	Waste heat recovery	Multiple	5–10	5–8	High	1–3	Commercialized	High

continued on next page

Table 6 *continued*

Overall Rank	Technology	Most Applicable Sector	Energy Savings Potential (%)	Ticket size (₹100,000)	Replication Potential (%)	Payback Period (years)	Market Acceptance	GHG Emission Reduction Potential
Industrial Energy Efficiency Technologies								
9.	IoT-based energy monitoring system	Multiple	20–35	1–10	High	3–4	Semi-commercialized	Medium
10.	Vapor absorption machine cooling system	Multiple	10–15	10–40	High	3–4	Commercialized	Low
11.	IE3/IE4 motors	Multiple	5–10	2–8	High	2–3	Commercialized	Medium
12.	Energy efficient star rated pump set	Multiple	20–30	2–10	High	2–3	Commercialized	Low
13.	Reduction steam leakage and use of steam traps	Multiple	25–30	1–20	High	2–3	Commercialized	Low
14.	Evaporative condenser for water cooling	Multiple	5–10	20–30	High	3–4	Commercialized	Low
15.	Forging presses with variable frequency drive	Forging	10–20	5–10	High	2–3	Commercialized	Low
16.	Co-generation boilers/gas engines	Multiple	10–30	150–400	Low	3–4	Semi-commercialized	Medium
17.	Microturbine	Chemicals/Textile/Paper	5–20	80–150	Medium	1–2	Commercialized	High
18.	CNC/VMC/Multi-axis machine	Engineering/Steel	20–30	20–35	Medium	3–4	Commercialized	Medium
19.	Reheating furnace and combustion control	Multiple	5–10	4–8	High	2–3	Commercialized	Low
20.	Screw air compressor	Multiple	15–20	2.5–10	High	1–2	Commercialized	Low
21.	PM motor air compressors	Multiple	25–30	10–20	High	1–2	Semi-commercialized	Low
22.	Falling film evaporator (Multi-effect)	Paper/Chemicals	10–20	200–400	Low	3–5	Semi-commercialized	Low
23.	Soft flow fabric dyeing machines	Textile	25–30	60–100	Medium	2–3	Commercialized	Low
24	Air jet loom for weaving	Textile	15–20	36–54	Medium	3–4	Commercialized	Low

continued on next page

Table 6 *continued*

Overall Rank	Technology	Most Applicable Sector	Energy Savings Potential (%)	Ticket size (₹100,000)	Replication Potential (%)	Payback Period (years)	Market Acceptance	GHG Emission Reduction Potential
Industrial Energy Efficiency Technologies								
25.	PLC automation jet dyeing machine	Textile	15–25	1–2	High	3–4	State of the art	Low
26.	BLDC fans	Multiple	40–50	1–2	Medium	2–3	Commercialized	Low
27.	EE stenter with waste heat recovery	Textile	20–30	100–200	Low	3–4	Semi-commercialized	High
28.	EE injection moulding machines with servo drives	Plastics	25–30	5–20	Medium	2–3	Commercialized	Medium
29.	Heat treatment – EE electrical furnaces with EnMS	Steel and allied sectors	10–20	3–10	Medium	2–4	Semi-commercialized	High
30.	High temperature fabric dyeing machine	Textile	15–30	60–90	Medium	3–4	Semi-commercialized	Low
31.	Insulation for furnace	Multiple	4–6	1–4	High	0–1	Commercialized	Low
32.	LSU dryer for rice mills	Food Processing	20–30	35–50	Medium	2–3	Semi-commercialized	Medium
33.	Multi-axis machining center	Engineering/ Steel	5–15	25–50	Medium	3–4	Commercialized	Low
34.	Water jet looms/ air jet weaving machine	Textile	5–15	30–45	Medium	3–5	Commercialized	Low
35.	Energy-efficient transformer	Multiple	20–70	1–10	Medium	2–3	Commercialized	Low
36.	Automatic vacuum hydraulic machine	Multiple	20–40	5–25	Medium	2–3	Commercialized	Low
37.	Solar steam generators/ water heaters	Multiple		20–100	Low	3–5	Commercialized	High
38.	Gasifier	Multiple	5–15	30–100	Medium	3–4	Semi-commercialized	Low
39.	Metal melting (divided blast cupola/gas cupola)	Foundry	15–20	20–30	Medium	2–3	Commercialized	Low
40.	Thermoforming sheet extrusion machine	Plastics	10–30	28–40	Medium	2–4	Commercialized	Low

continued on next page

Table 6 *continued*

Overall Rank	Technology	Most Applicable Sector	Energy Savings Potential (%)	Ticket size (₹100,000)	Replication Potential (%)	Payback Period (years)	Market Acceptance	GHG Emission Reduction Potential
				Industrial Energy Efficiency Technologies				
41.	Condensate heat recovery	Textile/ Paper/ Chemicals	10–30	2–5	Medium	2–3	Commercialized	Low
42.	Rotary screen-printing range	Textile	15–25	150–150	Low	3–4	Commercialized	Low
43.	Aluminum compressed air pipeline	Multiple	10–30	1–3	Medium	2–3	Commercialized	Low
44.	Automated core and sand plant	Foundry	5–10	100–300	Low	4–5	Semi-commercialized	Low
45.	Low thermal mass conveying system	Ceramics/ Steel	10–20	1–3	Medium	2–3	Commercialized	Low
46.	Optimization of compressed air control	Multiple	10–30	1–5	Medium	2–3	Commercialized	Low
47.	EE vacuum pump	Paper/ Chemicals	35–40	40–70	Low	3–4	Commercialized	Low
48.	Energy efficient blower/fans	Multiple	5–10	2–6	Medium	2–3	Commercialized	Low
49.	Automatic flat screen-printing machine	Textile	5–10	100–200	Low	3–4	Commercialized	Low
50.	Multi-layer film extruder	Plastics	35–50	30–30	Low	2–3	Commercialized	Medium
51.	Garment dyeing machines	Textile	25–30	60–60	Low	3–4	Commercialized	Low
52.	Thyristor-based control of electrical heaters	Multiple	5–15	1–5	Medium	2–3	Commercialized	Low
53.	Automatic power factor controller	Multiple	5–10	1–10	Medium	1–3	Commercialized	Low
54.	EE steam boiler with automation	Multiple	10–15	5–15	Medium	1–2	Commercialized	Low
55.	Yarn vacuum conditioning and heat setting systems	Textile	5–15	150–200	Low	3–5	Semi-commercialized	Low
56.	Scouring and bleaching	Textile	15–20	100–200	Low	3–4	Semi-commercialized	Low
57.	Rotating twin extruders	Plastics	15–20	50–50	Low	3–5	Commercialized	Low

continued on next page

Table 6 *continued*

Overall Rank	Technology	Most Applicable Sector	Energy Savings Potential (%)	Ticket size (₹100,000)	Replication Potential (%)	Payback Period (years)	Market Acceptance	GHG Emission Reduction Potential
Industrial Energy Efficiency Technologies								
58.	CSI and EE technologies in buildings (HVAC, chillers, building envelope, RE power, gas engines, LED lights and BLDC fans, IoT-based automations)	Commercial Buildings	5–35	15–1000	High	1–8	Commercialized	Medium
59.	CSI and EE technologies in buildings (HVAC, chillers, building envelope, RE power, gas engines, LED lights and BLDC fans, IoT-based automations)	Commercial Buildings	5–35	15–1000	High	1–8	Commercialized	Medium

BLDC = brushless direct current; EnMS = energy management system; HVAC = heating, ventilation, and air-conditioning; IE3/IE4 = International Efficiency; IGBT = Insulated Gate Bipolar Transistor; IoT = Internet of Things; LED = light emitting diode; LSU Louisiana State University; PLC = Programmable Logic Controller; VAM = vapor absorption machine; VMC = vertical machining centers.

[a] This will support energy transition: conversion from oil to electrically driven transport.

Sources: BEE energy audit reports; cluster profiles prepared under different assignments; reports on commercial buildings by CII, GBCI; multiple reports from NITI Aayog, etc. These have been validated during the consultations carried out with original equipment manufacturers, energy service companies, and third parties.

Technologies mapped in Table 6 cater to energy-intensive sectors and have energy savings potential of 5%–30%. Few technologies have higher energy savings potential of 50% or more.

In addition to the energy-intensive sectors identified, many of the commercialized technologies are crosscutting and support energy conservation in other SME sectors.

Commercialized technologies with medium and high payback have higher potential for financing, as these technologies are well-proven, and better financing solutions will support wider and faster adoption.

Commercialized technologies do not exhibit significant technical or performance risks and can be financed at scale through demand aggregation strategies.

Demand aggregation strategies can be supported by different players in the ecosystem to boost the economies of scale for commercialized technologies with lower ticket sizes. For example, Energy-Efficiency Services Limited (EESL), under the United Nations Industrial Development Organization- Global Environment Facility (UNIDO-GEF) project, is promoting the demand aggregation of the few industrial energy efficiency technologies such as variable frequency drives, jet dyeing machines, programmable logic computer-based automation, energy-efficient motors, and pump sets. EESL also has its own programs where it promotes demand aggregation of appliance related technologies such as light emitting diode (LED) light fixtures, brushless direct current and star labeled fans.

State-of-the-art technologies require a higher level of customization and can involve inherent technical and performance risks. Risk guarantee mechanisms can support the financial institutions to cover the associated risk enabling them to support the financing requirements of the SMEs.

Some of the semi-commercialized technologies with limited customization needs can be standardized for implementation and financing processes by providing due technical assistance to the implementing agencies and financial institutions. This can be implemented where the degree of customization required is higher, through project financing models with risk guarantee coverage along the lines of state-of-the-art technologies.

Based on the risk perception of financial institutions, semi-commercialized technologies can lend themselves either to standardization and demand aggregation strategies (like commercialized technologies) or to project financing with risk guarantee (like state-of-the-art technologies).

To capture the challenges and barriers before framing the solutions, it is important to map the supply chain for energy efficiency, CSI, and e-mobility technologies and draw on the key learnings from past programmatic interventions and the evolving policy landscape for developing better focused solutions.

Identifying the Most Promising E-Mobility Solutions

The Government of India has targeted around 30% electric vehicle penetration by 2030 (footnote 19). To achieve this target, there needs to be rapid transformational policies and measures that help pick up the pace of India's electric vehicle penetration. To increase the penetration of e-mobility at the ground level, it is imperative to understand the landscape of e-mobility in the country. While other countries have much more mature electric vehicle markets, the Indian electric vehicle market is still at its nascent stage. Some of the key factors that differentiate India's electric vehicle market from that of developed countries are as follows:

(i) The Indian consumer is still largely dependent on public transport (as of 2023, public transport has an oil-operated fleet) which includes buses, trains, three-wheeler automobiles, etc. for their day-to-day commute and travel. This is the key differentiating factor between India and other industrialized countries that have higher per capita income and are more developed.

(ii) With its limited infrastructure, the traffic density in the Indian metros and urban cities is higher than in industrialized countries.

(iii) The average Indian commutes around 5 kilometers (km) daily to reach their workplace, whereas, in the United States (US), this distance is approximately 26 km.

(iv) Since India is still a developing country, the average income of an Indian is much lower compared with the average income of its foreign counterparts in more developed countries. As a result, Indian consumers have generally low affordability and are price sensitive. For a price-sensitive customer, the most preferred vehicle category in the Indian transportation context is two-wheelers. Two-wheelers make up almost 80% of the total vehicle sales in the country. In India, the use of three-wheelers is also higher than in industrialized countries.

(v)   Being a price-sensitive economy with less than average income compared to developed countries, Indian consumers have overall lower vehicle ownership. For example, in 2018, data on vehicle ownership showed that India had 22 cars per 1,000 individuals, the US had around 980, and the United Kingdom had 850.[21]

It is anticipated that India's electric vehicle adoption will be led by two-wheelers and three-wheelers rather than four-wheelers. These vehicles are ideal for commuting short distances in cities and villages. They also have lower up-front costs compared to four-wheeler electric vehicles. It is also expected that the adoption of three-wheeler electric vehicles will be led by Indians to earn their livelihood. Three-wheeler electric vehicle solutions are expected to be the cheapest and safest solutions for last-mile connectivity of business-to-business and business-to-consumer businesses. Electric vehicles will play a key role in developing the shared mobility ecosystem in India. Since the operational cost of an electric vehicle is low, shared mobility will emerge as a highly cost-effective mode of transportation in the future. A 2021 study by NITI Aayog showed that an 80% electric vehicle penetration is expected for two-wheelers and three-wheelers by 2030, whereas around 50% electric vehicle penetration for four-wheelers and 30% electric vehicle penetration for buses are expected. To support the transition, a further investment of $3 billion is required to strengthen the electric vehicle charging infrastructure. Table 7 shows expected electric vehicle sales for each vehicle category by 2030 as per projections prepared by NITI Aayog.

Table 7: Electric Vehicle Sales (Actual and Projected)

Vehicle Category	Actual 2020 Sales	Projected 2030 Sales	Required Compound annual growth rate (%)	Potential ($ billion)
Two-Wheelers	89,000	56,594,000	91	91
Three-Wheelers	411,000	12,319,000	41	5
Four-Wheelers	15,000	10,587,000	92	73
Buses	600	542,000	98	8

Sources: Government of India, NITI Aayog and Deutsche Gesellschaft für Internationale Zusammenarbeit. 2021. *Status Quo Analysis of Various Segments of Electric Mobility and Low Carbon Passenger Road Transport in India.* New Delhi; projections carried out based by experts considering the assumptions for the e-mobility sector.

Figure 5 shows the total cost of ownership for different electric vehicles.[22]

These targets, if achieved, will result in savings of around 474 mtoe, which accounts for approximate savings of ₹15 trillion. With electric vehicles being a highly energy-efficient and green technology, the corresponding savings of carbon dioxide (CO_2) emissions is expected to be around 846 million tons per year.[23] E-mobility will support India to meet the NDCs and reduce the import dependency on oil and boost the growth of the sustainable economy.

[21]   N. Rampal. 2022. Only 8% Indian Families Own Cars, NFHS Finds. Over 50% Still Use Bicycles, Bikes & Scooters. *The Print.* 27 May.
[22]   P. Kumar and C. Kanuri. 2020. Total Cost of Ownership of Electric Vehicles: Implications for Policy and Purchase Decisions. *WRI INDIA.* 6 October.
[23]   Government of India, Public Information Bureau. 2019. NITI Aayog & RMI Release Technical Analysis of FAME II Scheme. Press release. 5 April.

Figure 5: Total Costs of Ownership of Electric Vehicles
(per kilometer)

Comparison of TCO per km

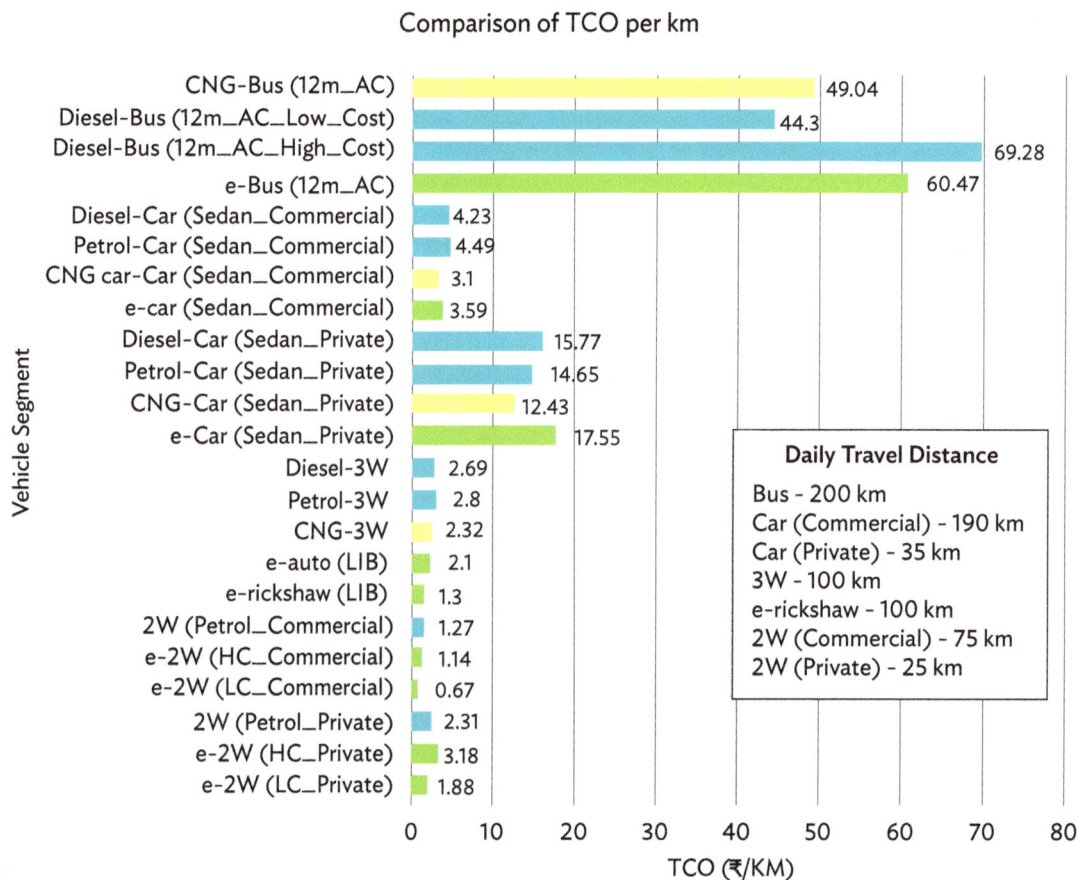

Vehicle Segment	TCO (₹/KM)
CNG-Bus (12m_AC)	49.04
Diesel-Bus (12m_AC_Low_Cost)	44.3
Diesel-Bus (12m_AC_High_Cost)	69.28
e-Bus (12m_AC)	60.47
Diesel-Car (Sedan_Commercial)	4.23
Petrol-Car (Sedan_Commercial)	4.49
CNG car-Car (Sedan_Commercial)	3.1
e-car (Sedan_Commercial)	3.59
Diesel-Car (Sedan_Private)	15.77
Petrol-Car (Sedan_Private)	14.65
CNG-Car (Sedan_Private)	12.43
e-Car (Sedan_Private)	17.55
Diesel-3W	2.69
Petrol-3W	2.8
CNG-3W	2.32
e-auto (LIB)	2.1
e-rickshaw (LIB)	1.3
2W (Petrol_Commercial)	1.27
e-2W (HC_Commercial)	1.14
e-2W (LC_Commercial)	0.67
2W (Petrol_Private)	2.31
e-2W (HC_Private)	3.18
e-2W (LC_Private)	1.88

Daily Travel Distance

Bus - 200 km
Car (Commercial) - 190 km
Car (Private) - 35 km
3W - 100 km
e-rickshaw - 100 km
2W (Commercial) - 75 km
2W (Private) - 25 km

₹ = rupee, 2W = two-wheeler, 3W = three-wheeler, AC = air-conditioned, CNG = compressed natural gas, e = electric, HC = high cost, km = kilometer, LC = low cost, LIB = lithium ion battery, m = meter, TCO = total cost of ownership.

Source: P. Kumar and C. Kanuri 2020. Total Cost of Ownership of Electric Vehicles: Implications for Policy and Purchase Decisions. WRI INDIA. 6 October.

4 SUPPLY CHAIN FOR ENERGY EFFICIENCY, CLIMATE-SMART INFRASTRUCTURE, AND E-MOBILITY TECHNOLOGIES

Energy Efficiency and Climate-Smart Infrastructure Supply Chain for Small and Medium-Sized Enterprises

The energy efficiency and CSI supply chain and ecosystem can be broadly categorized (i) OEM, (ii) local service provider (LSP), and (iii) energy service company (ESCO). Figure 6 shows various linkages among the different players working in the supply chain.

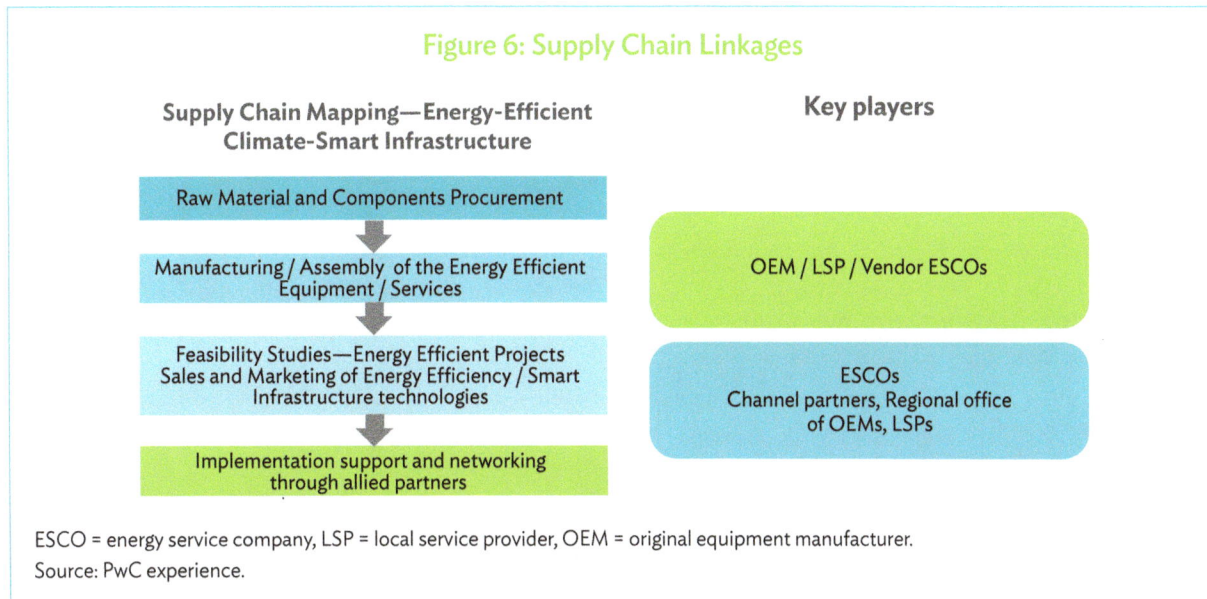

Figure 6: Supply Chain Linkages

Supply Chain Mapping—Energy-Efficient Climate-Smart Infrastructure

Key players

- Raw Material and Components Procurement
- Manufacturing / Assembly of the Energy Efficient Equipment / Services
- Feasibility Studies—Energy Efficient Projects Sales and Marketing of Energy Efficiency / Smart Infrastructure technologies
- Implementation support and networking through allied partners

OEM / LSP / Vendor ESCOs

ESCOs
Channel partners, Regional office of OEMs, LSPs

ESCO = energy service company, LSP = local service provider, OEM = original equipment manufacturer.
Source: PwC experience.

Original Equipment Manufacturers

Manufacturing facilities of OEMs to produce energy efficiency equipment and technology solutions are usually centralized at a few strategically selected locations based on the availability of the factors of production, and proximity to markets, etc (Box 1). They serve the clients through their regional and local sales offices or a usually elaborate network of channel partners that are locally available across the major SME clusters.

Box 1: Original Equipment Manufacturers

Some examples of OEMs actively working in the Indian energy efficiency CSI technology supply chain are

Thermax, SPG Prints, Voltas, Schneider Electric, ABB, Plasma Induction, Inductotherm, Jyoti CNC, Milacron, Kaeser Compressors, NCON Turbines, Cheema Boilers, etc.

These cover some of the key energy efficiency CSI technologies short-listed in chapter 2.

Source: PwC experience/Author analysis.

For instance, Inductotherm Corp.—a manufacturer of electric induction melting and heating technologies—has its manufacturing facility in Ahmedabad. Plasma Induction (India) Pvt. Ltd.—another OEM for this technology—has its manufacturing facility in Rajkot. They have regional teams and offices in all prominent SME clusters that utilize metal melting and heating operations (e.g., foundry and forging clusters across the country like Kolhapur, Coimbatore, Pune, etc.). These OEMs leverage the reach and expertise of their regional and local teams for sales and marketing of energy efficiency technologies.

(i)   An OEM is a crucial and integral part of the entire supply chain. **They manufacture and implement energy-efficient equipment and/or technologies and solutions for the industries**.

(ii) OEMs usually offer a wide spectrum of technology and solutions with the support of their extensive network of regional offices and/or channel partners. This may include standard off-the-shelf and fully commercialized energy efficiency technologies, as well as state-of-the-art modern technology solutions. OEMs may also manufacture tailored energy efficient equipment and/or solutions engineered to the specific requirements of SME customers and ESCOs working in the energy efficiency and CSI domain.

(iii) The large OEMs—especially with their significant sales pipelines through regional offices and channel partners—can leverage sales pipeline to drive energy efficiency and CSI finance by enticing the services of banks and/or NBFCs at the point of sale. This was validated by various OEMs during stakeholder consultations.

(iv) OEMs usually prefer the up-front payment (capital expenditure [capex] model) for implementation. The risk of the performance of the equipment is borne by the OEM against the design conditions.

(v)   Most of the technology suppliers have been working under the capex model with SMEs. Technology providers and/or OEMs (e.g., Schneider, Kaeser Compressors, Grundfos, etc.) that offer commercialized off-the-shelf energy efficiency products prefer to associate with channel partners for effective reach and local presence at SME clusters.

(vi) These technology providers support the capacity development of their channel partners through training programs and hand-holding support.

(vii) The OEMs who typically offer customizable solutions as part of their product range (e.g., Plasma, Thermax, Voltas, etc.) tend to operate through a network of regional and local offices in the SME clusters. These regional offices with technical experts provide the required support to the SMEs for sales and project execution.

(viii) Less than 5% of the large OEMs are led by women.[24] They have been conventionally led by males since the industrial revolution in India. However, with the rapid evolution of businesses, the stake of women in management and decision-making roles has been gradually increasing. Corporate OEMs like Cummins, Bosch, Schneider, Siemens, etc. have a higher percentage of the female workforce along with a few other SME OEMs. For instance, Plasma is one of the women-led OEMs providing sustainable energy efficiency products.

(ix) The building sector has women leaders who are leading the forms and institutions for defining new norms for sustainable and climate-friendly growth of the building sector. GBCI India is a women-led organization.

The execution of energy efficiency and CSI technology solutions also requires access to finance. Smaller OEMs require working capital loans for the execution of large-scale energy efficiency projects, while SMEs obtain finance mostly as term loans for the implementation of technology solutions. Leading OEMs also have tie-ups with NBFCs to ease the financing requirements for the SME units and to provide innovative financing arrangements including leasing. Financing institutions have an important role to play in the clean energy adoption and transition at SMEs.

---

[24]   Based on multiple consultations the value is estimated.

Energy efficiency solutions vary from $100 to a few thousand dollars. Based on the ticket size and their individual needs, the SME procures the equipment through self-financing, working capital financing, or term loans. Third-party financing plays a crucial role in fostering the adoption of modern energy efficiency and CSI technologies. **NBFCs and financial institutions have the expertise in evaluating energy efficiency and CSI and will play a crucial role in the long run**.

Local Service Providers

LSPs are one of the crucial parts of the supply chain of the energy efficiency and CSI technology network (Box 2). LSPs are present locally in specific SME clusters and regions and provide energy efficiency solutions in the specific clusters. They have a limited geographical presence and usually cater to customized solutions and requirements of the specific MSME sectors located in the region or cluster. For instance, EnEFF provides energy efficiency furnaces for forging and heat treatment applications to the SME industrial requirement in and around Ludhiana.

> ### Box 2: Local Service Providers
>
> Some examples of LSPs actively working in the Indian energy efficiency and CSI supply chain are Basotra Engineers, EnEFF furnaces, Airprax Pneumatics, ISCT, Channel partners of OEMs, Local Fabricators, etc.
>
> Source: PwC experience/Author analysis.

LSPs usually prefer the capital expenditure model for implementation. Investment in energy efficiency and CSI solutions varies from a few thousand dollars to less than $12,500. Most of the solutions offered by LSPs have lower payback periods, and SMEs generally do not opt for institutional finance for implementation of these energy efficiency solutions. Working capital limits available with the present banker are also used by SMEs for the implementation of these solutions.

Channel partners of the large OEMs working in the SME cluster would require working capital finance for the execution of energy efficiency projects. Typically, these channel partners are themselves SMEs. A few LSPs provide bank guarantees as a payment security mechanism while working with large OEMs during the execution of energy efficiency and CSI projects.

Key Supply Chain Challenges that Persist in the Energy Efficiency and CSI Supply Chain

Addressing the complexities of the energy efficiency and CSI supply chain involves tackling several persistent challenges. These challenges underscore the sector's dependence on imported components for sophisticated machinery and automation, limited outreach of technology providers to smaller clusters, and barriers in integrating smart technologies like IoT and Industry 4.0. Furthermore, the shortage of skilled personnel and the absence of robust frameworks for measurement and verification pose additional hurdles in scaling up adoption across diverse sectors. Some of these challenges include:

(i) dependence on the import of the components for energy efficiency equipment and import dependence for large, sophisticated machinery, high-end sensors for automation (such as permanent magnets for motors, specialized castings for pumps and valves, electronic components and sensors for automation, high-end technologies for productivity enhancement, etc.).

(ii) limited reach of energy efficiency technology providers to smaller clusters.

(iii) limited penetration of smart technologies (IoT, Industry 4.0, energy management system) and historical data requirement for customization of energy efficiency solutions.

(iv) lack of local availability of skilled personnel for execution and operation of energy efficiency technologies (limits the adoption of the new technologies in least-advanced SME clusters only).

(v) lack of adequate framework for measurement and verification (M&V) activities for performing the guaranteed test for energy efficient equipment (highly customizable and state-of-the-art technologies require the M&V framework to prove the energy savings).

Major Challenges Resulting in Lower Adoption of Energy Efficiency Technologies in SMEs

The adoption of energy efficiency technologies among SMEs faces significant barriers that hinder their widespread implementation. These challenges include perceived high costs, lack of awareness and confidence in energy efficiency technologies, limited access to financing, and concerns regarding the techno-economic feasibility of these solutions within SME operations.

(i) Around 70% of the technology providers responded that the higher cost of equipment and lack of awareness or confidence in energy efficiency technologies (and the resulting limited demand for energy efficiency and CSI equipment) among SMEs are major hurdles to the adoption of energy efficiency technologies in MSMEs. Only a few of the respondents confirmed that they assist MSMEs to get finance from financial institutions and NBFCs during the procurement stage. A lack of financing for MSMEs delays the wider adoption of energy efficiency measures (Figure 7).

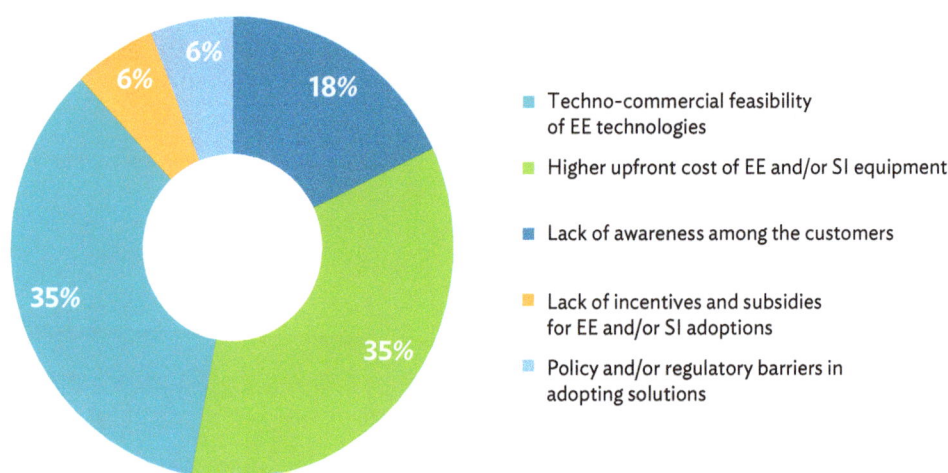

Figure 7: Reasons for Lower Adoption of Energy Efficiency Technologies Among Micro, Small, and Medium-Sized Enterprises

- Techno-commercial feasibility of EE technologies
- Higher upfront cost of EE and/or SI equipment
- Lack of awareness among the customers
- Lack of incentives and subsidies for EE and/or SI adoptions
- Policy and/or regulatory barriers in adopting solutions

EE = energy efficiency, SI = smart infrastructure.
Source: Based on 12 consultations through discussion guides carried out during the study.

(ii) Around 18% of the OEMs consulted indicated the limited techno-economic feasibility of energy efficiency technologies at SMEs and a lack of capabilities to evaluate the allied benefits of energy efficiency technologies as barriers that hinder the implementation of capital-intensive technologies in MSMEs.

Business Models Preferred by Original Equipment Manufacturers and Local Service Providers

(i) Around **77% of the technology providers operate on the capex model (up-front payment for a purchase)**. The following risks related to the SME sector also contribute to this trend:

(a) Low credibility of SMEs to repay.

    (b)   Limited opportunities for M&V assessment in MSME units.

    (c)   Challenges in energy baseline assessments.

(ii)   **Less than 8% of the OEMs consulted during the study also offer leasing-based financing solutions for their customers** through special arrangements with financial institutions. OEMs that responded to this question provided commercialized solutions, and these technologies have good resale value and have access to a secondary market for resale. Some of the leading NBFCs and financial institutions actively supporting this model are Siemens Financial Services, Electronica Finance Limited (EFL), etc. Most of the equipment financed and executed under this model have a good secondhand market and/or are backed by appropriate buyback guarantees from the OEM that help financial

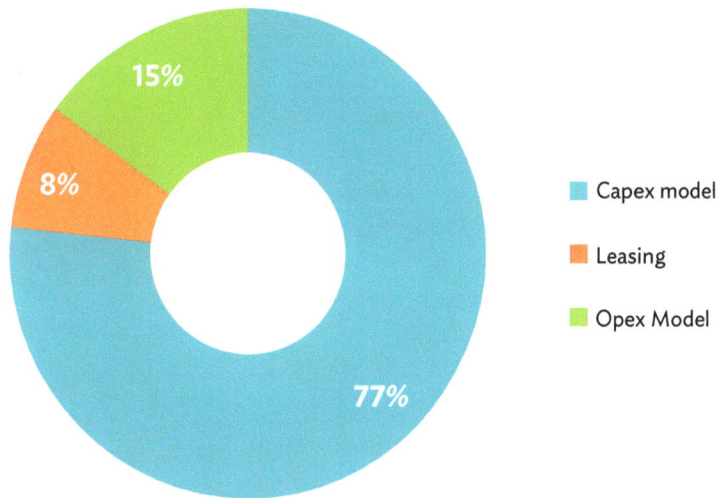

Figure 8: Preferred Business Models

- Capex model
- Leasing
- Opex Model

15%

8%

77%

capex = capital expenditure, opex = operating expenses.
Source: Based on stakeholder consultations carried out during the study.

institutions moderate the risk of default by MSMEs.

(iii) **Around 15% of the respondents provide opex-based solutions (leasing and/or service-based payment mechanism).** CSI and renewable energy solution providers usually use a hybrid mode, where some percentage of the payment is taken up front, and the rest of the payments are linked to long-term service agreements. OEMs take the loan on their balance sheet for the execution of the assignments (Figure 8).

Women Working as Employees or Value Chain Partners in Clean Energy Enterprises

Traditionally, women have been understated as employees within the clean energy landscape, particularly in technology and engineering-related roles. The inclusion of women in tech-oriented roles within the clean energy sector will not only help generate more employment opportunities but will also create a better understanding of customer needs to design and create more gender-inclusive products and services.[25]

---

[25]   Details of women's presence in the supply chain are presented in Appendix 3.

Companies such as Dharma Life, Frontier Markets, etc. working in the energy efficiency space have smoothly incorporated women—especially rural women—as their product distributors and sales agents in villages and other rural parts of the country. Dharma Life's sustainable products such as solar lights, clean cookstoves, etc. have reached 10 million beneficiaries across more than 50,000 villages in 13 states of India through its network of over 16,000 rural women entrepreneurs.

To enable participation from women entrepreneurs in the last-mile delivery segment, they must have support from other family members, businesses must provide them with the requisite training and safe working timing and conditions, etc. to easily commute and build a strong customer base to generate a viable income.

Energy Service Company

An energy service company (ESCO) forms a critical link in the energy efficiency supply chain. ESCOs are responsible for energy audits, preparing detailed investment grade project reports, procuring equipment, project implementation, and monitoring evaluations. ESCOs provide the technical support required by SMEs to understand energy efficiency solutions (Box 3).

ESCOs are mostly situated in the metro regions, including Pune, Delhi NCR, and Bengaluru. Vendor ESCOs have central manufacturing facilities and operate through marketing and services teams across the different SME clusters, e.g., prominent ESCOs in Pune region include Yantra Harvest, Saven, and SWID. Vendor ESCOs such as Promethean, Bosch, and Schneider have corporate offices in Bengaluru region. **Few ESCOs in India are led by women as partners or directors**.

> ### Box 3: Energy Service Companies
>
> Some examples of pure energy service companies actively working in the Indian energy efficiency and climate-smart infrastructure technology supply chain are Smart Joules, Yantra Harvest, Servotech Power, Cosmoright Services Pvt. Ltd, Desire Energy, Power Tech, SWID, Alien Energy, etc.
>
> Source: PwC experience / Author analysis.

ESCOs can be broadly categorized into two categories: pure ESCOs and vendor ESCOs.

(i)   **Pure ESCOs** provide service-oriented solutions such as energy audits, preparing detailed investment grade project reports, support in procurement of equipment, energy efficiency project implementation, and monitoring or evaluation of resulting energy savings. Pure ESCO companies do not manufacture but source equipment and technologies from OEMs. ESCOs are concentered in the metro regions (e.g., Alien Energy, Smart Joule) and prominent MSME clusters (e.g., Yantra Harvest, Saven, SWID). ESCOs work closely with MSME and technology providers for the execution of ESCO projects in industries and buildings. They are positioned to be among the most effective enablers for demand aggregation as they work very closely with multiple MSMEs and buildings to support energy efficiency and CSI technologies. However, they are often limited in the size and extent of their operations. They usually originate as service sector start-ups and can scale their operations to varying degrees.

(ii) **Vendor ESCOs** are an integral part of the energy efficiency and CSI supply chain. They are engaged in the design and manufacture of energy efficiency and CSI technologies like their larger counterpart OEMs. They often are start-ups or operate at a smaller scale compared to large OEMs. In addition to the manufacture of technologies or equipment, they provide solutions and services around energy performance guarantees and performance contracting, like those offered by ESCOs. **Vendor ESCOs offer high-end customizable energy efficiency solutions and state-of-the-art technologies based on unit-level parameters. Vendor ESCOs carry out an in-depth study of the processes, defining baseline, and M&V protocols using data monitoring, and carry out the implementation on partially capex and ESCO models**.

Understanding the Key Challenges Faced by Suppliers and Energy Service Companies

Based on multiple interactions with different suppliers, the study mapped the business models adopted by different suppliers.

In addition to inputs for the long list of energy efficiency and CSI technologies for MSMEs, the consultations helped the study to understand the various challenges related to energy efficiency financing in MSMEs. These technology providers serve as the first avenue to understand cluster dynamics such as local industry energy efficiency technology needs, market trends, adoption levels, and barriers toward energy efficiency.

The study conducted 12 consultations with OEMs and technology providers. The study asked questions regarding the preferred mode of implementation in the MSME sector, outreach to MSME clusters, and reasons for the lower adoption of energy efficiency technologies in MSMEs.

Figure 9: Major Hurdles for Energy Services Companies

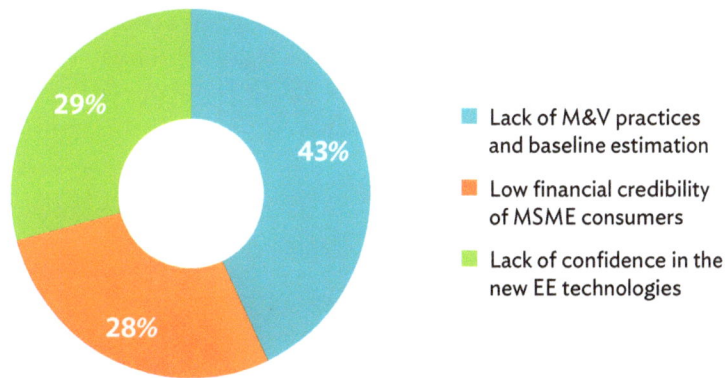

- Lack of M&V practices and baseline estimation — 43%
- Low financial credibility of MSME consumers — 28%
- Lack of confidence in the new EE technologies — 29%

EE = energy efficiency; M&V = measurement and verification; MSME = micro, small, and medium-sized enterprise.
Source: This is based on stakeholder discussions as per the original report.

Major Hurdles Faced by Energy Service Companies

Less than half of the ESCOs (43%) responded that the lack of standard M&V protocols for ESCO projects is the key hurdle in assessing the energy efficiency potential of the projects (Figure 9).[26] ESCOs advised that a better regulatory and legal system, along with strict M&V protocols, can boost ESCO projects in the country. Programmatic interventions around technical assistance support for M&V will be rolled out for developing the ecosystem and culture of energy efficiency in the industries and developing the M&V framework for ESCO projects.[27]

(i) Few ESCOs prefer to use IoT-enabled platforms for evaluating real-time energy savings for easier M&V processes. This requires the metering of multiple parameters and so is limited to the upper end of the medium-sized units that possess multiple metering points in the units.

(ii) Almost all ESCOs have confirmed that long lead times and high transaction costs associated with energy studies and baseline estimation are the major challenges for the execution of energy efficiency projects in MSMEs and remained the main hurdle for executing ESCO-based projects.

---

[26] Alliance for an Energy Efficient Economy (AEEE). 2020. *Transforming the Energy Services Sector in India Towards a Billion Dollar ESCO Market*.
[27] This is based on stakeholder discussions as per the original report.

(iii)   All the ESCOs consulted responded that access to lower cost of funds is the major hurdle. Only a few responded that they can seek project financing from some NBFCs. Other ESCOs only have access to balance sheet-based financing for ESCO projects.

Business Models Preferred by Energy Service Companies

(i)   Pure ESCOs and vendor ESCOs prefer the **guaranteed savings model** in the absence of project finance or third-party loans. In a guaranteed savings model, an ESCO receives the agreed fee from the utility or owner once the savings are proven through a rigorous measurement and verification process. Payment of ESCO fees is based on the savings achieved. If no savings are achieved, no payments would be due to the ESCO.

(ii)   The **shared savings model** is preferred by an ESCO when project finance is available (term loan or line of credit) to meet the financing requirements of the energy efficiency and CSI implementation. A few niche NBFCs with the ability to evaluate energy efficiency and CSI projects support the ESCOs with financing solutions for the wider uptake of the energy efficiency and CSI loans. The shared savings model is when an ESCO and/or company installs energy-saving equipment and verifies or establishes the energy savings through a measurement and verification framework. Based on the monetary savings achieved, the ESCO is paid a percentage share of the savings within an agreed period for the duration of the contract. No up-front payment is made to the ESCO. The above findings are based on five stakeholder consultations carried out during the study.

Figure 10: Supply Chain of E-mobility

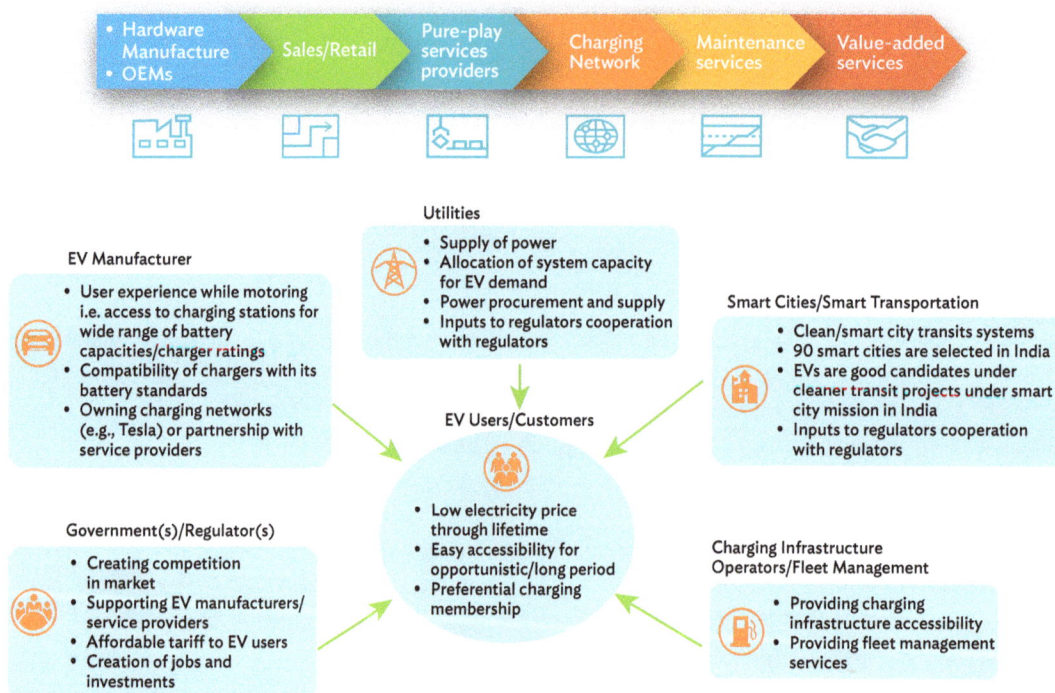

EV = electric vehicle, OEM = original equipment manufacturer.
Source: PwC project experience.

Figure 11: Value Chain of Electric Mobility

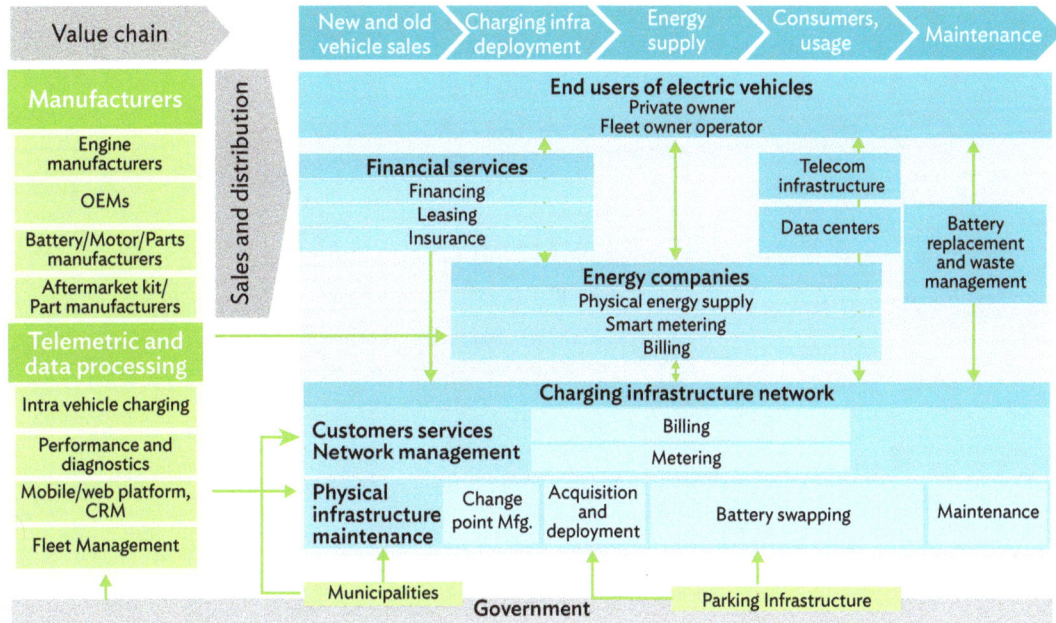

CRM = customer relationship management, mfg = manufacturing, OEM = original equipment manufacturer.
Source: PwC project experience.

Understanding the E-mobility Supply Chain in India

Within the e-mobility value chain, several key stakeholders play an important role as key enablers in India's transition to zero-emission mobility. Broadly, these stakeholders fall into one or more of the following categories: funding providers, regulation providers, and knowledge providers. Figure 10 shows the electric vehicle landscape in India along with the roles of its key stakeholders. Figure 11 shows how the different stakeholders are interconnected across the entire value chain.

There are several upcoming and innovative business models across the globe within the electric vehicle ecosystem. These business models are designed to address various challenges that are inhibiting the adoption of electric vehicles, such as high up-front cost, apprehension around battery life, battery charging time, and range anxiety.

Table 8 describes various business models that exist in India within the e-mobility landscape.

Apart from the key business models in Table 8, several new and innovative business models have emerged across the e-mobility value chain within the evolving landscape of India's electric mobility.

Table 8: Electric Vehicle Business Models and Ecosystem

Business Model	Description	Prominent Players
Vehicle Leasing Model	• Vehicles are leased on a monthly rental basis allowing the customer to use the vehicle without owning it. • The model aims to solve the problem of high up-front cost of electric vehicles. • These schemes are specially designed to cater to the customer anxiety related to owning a vehicle as it takes care of the insurance, maintenance, registration, taxes, etc.	Autovert, ETO Motors, Orix Auto, Myles, Mahindra Finance
Battery Leasing Model	• The Government of India issued a new regulation that allowed electric vehicle manufacturers to sell the vehicle without a battery. • This model allows the consumer to lease the battery on a monthly rental or subscription model bringing down the high up-front cost of an electric vehicle.	Esmito, Sun Mobility, Ampere Electric
Battery Swapping Model	• This business model essentially serves as an extension of the above-mentioned battery leasing model that allows customers to swap a drained or used battery with a fully charged battery by paying a certain fixed fee. • The success of this model depends on developing a well-connected network of swapping stations that can help in addressing the range anxiety of customers.	Battery Smart, VoltUp, ChargeUp, Charge+Zone
Charging Infrastructure Providers	• Charging infrastructure providers follow a "charging-as-a-service" (CaaS model) that allows customers to charge their vehicles either on a subscription-based model or a pay-per-use model. This business model is highly capital-intensive and has limited geographic penetration as of 2023.	TATA Power, Panasonic, Exicom, Fortum India

Note: "Range anxiety" is a commonly used term in the electric vehicle ecosystem. It refers to the apprehension of the electric vehicle owner that the vehicle's battery will run out of power before completing the journey or a suitable charging point is reached.

Source: Consultations with original equipment manufacturers.

E-mobility Suppliers

Based on the short-listed electric vehicle and e-mobility technologies, suppliers have been identified (Appendix 4). The study reached out to multiple e-mobility players. The consultations helped the study to understand the supply chain dynamics; risk assigned at different levels; and what works and what does not for a particular technology such as investor confidence, reliability, adoption levels, payback period, etc.

Based on multiple interactions with different suppliers, the study mapped challenges and possible solutions.[28]

---

[28] Five consultations were conducted with OEMs, technology providers, and service providers from the e-mobility sector.

Major Challenges and Barriers Faced by the Different Players in the E-mobility Ecosystem

The e-mobility sector confronts a multitude of challenges and barriers impacting various stakeholders. Addressing these issues is crucial for fostering broader adoption and sustainability within the electric vehicle market. Some of these challenges include:

(i)   import dependence on the batteries and components required for electric vehicles;

(ii)   lack of an adequate ecosystem of charging infrastructure required for the wider adoption of electric vehicles;

(iii)   limited range of electric vehicles and a higher initial cost of the vehicle;

(iv)   charging infrastructure business model is unviable (i.e., having a poor internal rate of return) in present and immediate future scenarios;

(v)   resale risk (absence of a strong secondary market);

(vi)   high up-front cost of electric vehicles i.e., higher up-front cash outflow compared to ICE vehicles (higher interest rates, low loan tenure, low loan-to-value ratio); and

(vii)   higher insurance costs compared to ICE vehicles.

Key Outcomes and Probable Solutions That Can Support E-mobility

Some critical steps toward enhancing the affordability, accessibility, and sustainability of electric vehicles include:

(i)   All players working in the e-mobility ecosystem should emphasize the need to strengthen the policy intervention around reusing, leasing, and recycling batteries to make electric vehicles more affordable.

(ii)   Apply blended finance schemes for lowering the cost of financing will support the development of a long-term sustainable solution for prompting the penetration of e-mobility.

(iii)   Policies or regulations that can support cost reductions related to land purchase or leasing for developing the e-charging infrastructure should be introduced.

(iv)   Use a risk guarantee mechanism that can support the larger deployment of the e-mobility ecosystem.

(v)   Promote research and development institutes for developing the new age energy storage solutions.

Women's Empowerment through E-mobility Initiatives

ETO Motors—one of India's leading electric mobility service providers—announced its collaboration with the Delhi Metro, together with the support of the GMR Varalakshmi foundation and MOWO, a nongovernment organization promoting safe mobility for women. As part of the agreement, around 300 women drivers will be deployed across various metro stations located in the Delhi NCR region to provide last-mile connectivity to commuters through ETO's sustainable and environmentally friendly e-rickshaws. ETO's electric vehicle charging stations are strategically located at various metro stations, residential societies, and other public places to enable easy access to vehicle chargers for women drivers. Further, MOWO will be responsible for the onboarding and training of women, and the entire initiative will be focused toward providing continued guidance and support to women to help them become micro-entrepreneurs, increasing their employability.[29]

---

[29]   ETO Motors Pvt Ltd. n.d. Electric Mobility Solutions in India – ETO Motors.

5 ANALYZING THE SCHEMES AND POLICIES LANDSCAPE

In the context of the MSME sector, energy efficiency financing is inherently considered risky for financial institutions to support because of uncertainties associated with the performance of technology interventions (especially semi-commercialized and state-of-the-art) and the difficulty in demonstrating the savings.

Various financing schemes have been introduced to promote MSMEs and energy efficiency with a focus on promoting energy efficiency-centric financing in MSMEs.

A single financial scheme cannot eliminate all the barriers faced by MSMEs availing of finance to support energy efficiency-enhancing projects. Several schemes have been designed which eliminate a few of the risks. Figure 12 shows a broad classification of the financing schemes supporting MSMEs in India.[30]

Figure 12: Financing Schemes Supporting Micro, Small, and Medium-Sized Enterprises in India

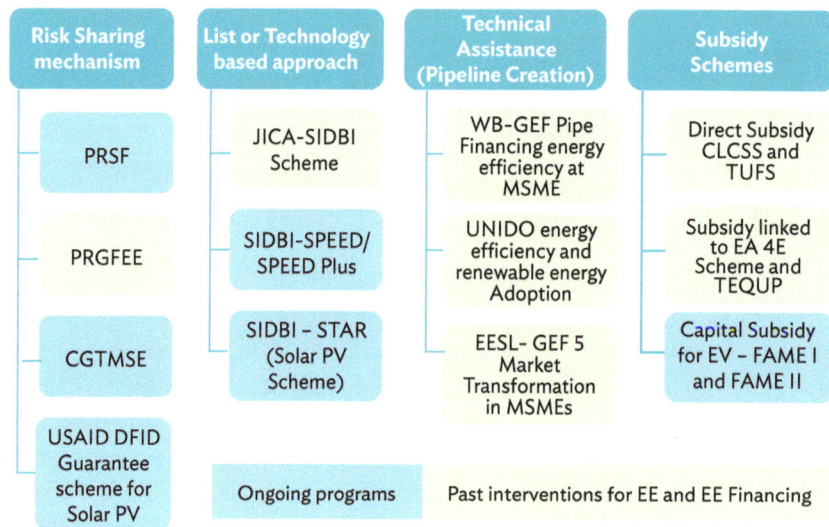

Risk Sharing mechanism	List or Technology based approach	Technical Assistance (Pipeline Creation)	Subsidy Schemes
PRSF	JICA-SIDBI Scheme	WB-GEF Pipe Financing energy efficiency at MSME	Direct Subsidy CLCSS and TUFS
PRGFEE	SIDBI-SPEED/ SPEED Plus	UNIDO energy efficiency and renewable energy Adoption	Subsidy linked to EA 4E Scheme and TEQUP
CGTMSE	SIDBI – STAR (Solar PV Scheme)	EESL- GEF 5 Market Transformation in MSMEs	Capital Subsidy for EV – FAME I and FAME II
USAID DFID Guarantee scheme for Solar PV			

Ongoing programs   Past interventions for EE and EE Financing

4E = end to end energy efficiency; CGTMSE = Credit Guarantee Fund Trust for Micro and Small Enterprises; CLCSS = Credit Linked Capital Subsidy Scheme; DFID = Department for International Development of the United Kingdom; EA = energy audit; EE = energy efficiency; EESL = Energy Efficiency Services Limited; EV = electric vehicle; FAME = Faster Adoption and Manufacturing of (Hybrid and) Electric Vehicles; GEF = Global Environment Facility; JICA = Japan International Cooperation Agency; MSMEs = micro, small, and medium-sized enterprises; PRGFEE = Partial Risk Guarantee Fund for Energy Efficiency; PRSF = partial risk sharing facility; PV = photovoltaic; SIDBI = Small Industries Development Bank of India; TEQUP = Technology Upgradation Scheme for Micro, Small, and Medium Enterprises; TUFS = Technology Upgradation Funding Scheme; UNIDO = United Nations Industrial Development Organization; USAID = United States Agency for International Development; WB = World Bank.

Sources: PwC project experience; consultations carried out during the course of the project.

---

30   Various state initiatives and allied benefits for the different sectors is presented in Appendix 5.

Table 9 summarizes key features of different financing schemes.

Table 9: Key Features of Different Financing Schemes

Financing Scheme	Incentives/ Subsidies	Line of Credit (including Revolving Funds)	Risk Guarantee	Technical Assistance (including Environmental Assessments and Capacity Building)	Energy Service Company Implementation	Awareness Creation Activities
Partial Risk Guarantee Fund for Energy Efficiency Only shared savings (ESCO-based financing)			✓✓	✓✓	✓✓✓	✓
Partial Risk Sharing Facility Both shared savings and guaranteed savings			✓✓	✓✓	✓✓✓	✓
Credit Guarantee Fund Trust for Micro and Small Enterprises			✓✓✓			
JICA – SIDBI LoC for MSME EE technologies	✓✓	✓				✓
SPEED and SPEED PLUS	✓✓					
WB-GEF Financing EE at MSMEs		P		✓✓✓		PP
UNIDO-GEF EE RE Adoption in MSMEs		P		✓✓✓		✓✓
Promoting Market Transformation for EE in MSMEs		P		✓✓	✓✓✓	✓✓
Technology Upgradation Scheme for Micro Small and Medium Enterprises	✓✓			PP		P
4E scheme (end to end energy efficiency)	✓✓	✓		PP		✓
Technology Upgradation Funding Scheme	✓✓✓					
Credit Linked Capital Subsidy Scheme	✓✓✓					
Fame I and II	✓✓✓					✓✓
USAID DFID			✓✓✓			

4E = end to end energy efficiency, DFID = Department for International Development of the United Kingdom, EE = energy efficiency, ESCO = energy savings company, GEF = Global Environment Facility, JICA = Japan International Cooperation Fund, LoC = line of credit, MSME = micro, small, and medium-sized enterprises, RE = renewable energy, SIDBI = Small Industries Development Bank of India, UNIDO = United Nations Industrial Development Organization, USAID = United States Agency for International Development, WB = World Bank.

Source: Consultant's research work and stakeholder consultations.

Risk Guarantee Schemes

A major issue that lenders face while financing MSMEs is the lack of indemnity on the part of MSMEs concerning the successful completion of the loan cycle. Risk-sharing schemes are designed so that this issue is significantly addressed. The uncertainty related to repayments is covered by risk-sharing facilities (guarantee funds and first-loss facilities) either through a guarantee or first-loss absorption. Details of these schemes are presented in Appendix 5.

The Credit Guarantee Fund Trust for Micro and Small Enterprises (CGTMSE) was launched to promote the MSME sector by providing financial assistance for availing a loan of up to $250,000 without any collateral or third-party guarantee. The Small Industries Development Bank of India (SIDBI) is the nodal agency for the implementation of the scheme, which is promoted by over 125 empaneled financial institutions and NBFCs. It offers additional incremental risk coverage to women entrepreneurs. **Under this scheme, women-led firms are eligible for 80% of the credit risk for loan amounts up to $250,000** (Appendix 5).

The partial risk sharing facility (PRSF) and the now withdrawn **Partial Risk Guarantee Fund for Energy Efficiency (PRGFEE)** are two risk-sharing mechanisms supporting energy efficiency financing in India. These schemes provide financial institutions with partial coverage of the risk involved in extending loans for energy efficiency projects implemented under the performance contracting model. The risk-sharing facility encourages financial institutions to expand into new markets that are perceived to be risky and less proven energy efficiency technologies.

The relatively low uptake of the scheme can be attributed to the unavailability of a robust ecosystem for ESCO players, rigorous documentation, procedures (including the need for energy audit and M&V for each loan case being perceived as tedious), low awareness, and some aspects of the operating mechanisms of the schemes, among others.

The United States Agency for International Development (USAID) and the Development Finance Corporation (DFC) partnered with New York-based Encourage Capital—an environmentally focused investment firm—and two Indian NBFCs—**cKers Financial and woman-owned Electronica Finance Limited (EFL)**—to address challenges of risk associated with the implementation of solar photovoltaics by the SME sector.

Table 10: Summary of Key Risk Guarantee Schemes

Name of Risk Guarantee Schemes	Duration	Total Budget ($ million)	Uptake of the Scheme	Financial Institutions involved	% of Risk guaranteed	Eligible loan size ($ million)	EE/CSI/ EV
CGTMSE	2000– Ongoing		High	126	75–85	0.2	EE
PRGFEE[a]	2016–2021	39	No Uptake	5	50	1.25	EE / RE
PRSF	2015– Ongoing	34.3	Limited uptake	14	75	1.9	EE
USAID DFID Guarantee scheme for Solar photovoltaics	2021– Ongoing	34.9	Recently Launched	2	Case-by-case basis		CSI (RE)

CGTMSE = Credit Guarantee Fund Trust for Micro and Small Enterprises, CSI = climate-smart infrastructure, DFID = Department for International Development of the United Kingdom, EE = energy efficiency, EV = electric vehicle, PRGFEE = Partial Risk Guarantee fund for Energy Efficiency, PRSF = partial risk sharing facility, RE = renewable energy, USAID = United States Agency for International Development.

[a] The scheme was withdrawn and details are presented on past programs on energy efficiency in Appendix 5.

Sources: CGTMSE annual report 2020; Partial Risk Guarantee Fund for Energy Efficiency; Partial Risk Sharing Facility; USAID-DFID scheme.

Key Features and Challenges

The **key features** of risk guarantee schemes aim to transform lending practices from traditional collateral-based approaches to project-based financing models. These schemes, facilitated through energy saving performance contracts like Energy Service Performance Contracting (ESPC), ensure both the techno-commercial viability of projects and mitigate barriers faced by ESCOs in accessing financing.

(i) The scheme attempts to reorient the lender perspective from **collateral-based lending to project-based financing**.

(ii) Energy saving performance contracts (Energy Service Performance Contracting [ESPC]) (ESCO detailed project report [DPR]) **ensure the techno-commercial viability of the project** and promotes project-based financing.

(iii) Reducing the barriers faced by ESCOs in availing of financing, **enables ESCOs by providing a loan** and in turn can serve as project implementors.

The **key challenges** of risk guarantee schemes include:

(i) Lack of ecosystem for ESCO uptake. Only a handful of the registered ESCOs provide the entire spectrum of services. No incentives and tax breaks on implementing ESCO projects. Also lack of regulation for ESPC contracting and M&V protocols.

(ii) Long lead time and transaction cost. ESCO implementations require energy study at MSME, which increases the lead time and transaction costs.

(iii) No direct financial benefits for MSMEs such as interest subsidies limit uptake.

Detailed observations of the schemes are presented in Appendix 6.

USAID and the DFC announced that they are jointly sponsoring a $50 million loan portfolio guarantee to Kotak Mahindra Bank to support increased access to finance for women borrowers, and MSMEs across India.

This program will play a crucial role in women's economic empowerment as at least 50% of the loans are earmarked to be lent to women-led or women-managed MSMEs, or MSMEs that employ a certain percentage of women or that produce a good or service that disproportionately benefits women. It is likely to benefit more than 30,000 individual women borrowers and 7,500 MSME firms.

List-Based and Technology Approaches

The list-based approach for financing energy efficiency has seen a lot of traction in India. The unique selling proposition of the list-based approach is that it is easy to understand and implement from financial institutions and MSMEs perspective. In this approach, a list of commercialized technologies that have a significant energy savings potential—usually 10% or more—is selected for financing by providing an extensive list of eligible energy efficient equipment. This approach helps reduce transaction costs and ensures faster processing of loans and implementation of energy efficiency projects. The **Japan International Cooperation Agency (JICA) and SIDBI have successfully adopted this approach for energy efficiency and equipment financing**.

Capital subsidy schemes are non-recurring financial support from the government to the beneficiaries. These schemes tend to decrease the cost of investment on the side of the investor (here, it is the MSME). This type of support is usually popular among the beneficiaries. The capital subsidy schemes designed for MSMEs in India are not exclusively focused on energy efficiency. **FAME II** is focused on promoting the development of the ecosystem for e-mobility in the country.

Table 11: Key List-Based and Technology Approaches

Name of List-Based Schemes	Duration	Interest Rates (%)	Key Features	Quantum of Assistance	Loan Tenure	EE / CSI / EV
SIDBI Speed Plus	2019–Ongoing	8.8–10.5	Collateral free loans	100% of the machine cost $0.25 million for new customer	2–5 years	EE
SIDBI term loan for Roof Top	2019–Ongoing	9.1–10.2	100% finance, 0% equity required	$0.3 million	5 years	RE
JICA - SIDBI[a]	2009–2018	5.0–8.5	Interest Subsidy (0.5% to 2% during different phase of the program)	900 EE equipment eligible for financing developed under the scheme with interest sub-invention	NA	EE / RE
FAME I and FAME II[b]	2015–2024 (Ongoing)	NA	Capital subsidy of 40% of the cost of the vehicle (Over 160 models of EV are eligible for subsidy)	Over 303,000 vehicles incentivized under the FAME scheme and incentives of over $138 million disbursed under FAME II until FY2022	3–6 years	EV and EV-charging

CSI = climate-smart infrastructure, EE = energy efficiency, EV = electric vehicle, FAME = Faster Adoption and Manufacturing of (Hybrid and) Electric Vehicles, FY = fiscal year, JICA = Japan International Cooperation Agency, NA = not applicable, SIDBI = Small Industries Development Bank of India.

[a] The scheme was withdrawn and details are presented on past programs on energy efficiency in Appendix 5.
[b] Government of India, Ministry of Heavy Industries. FAME India Scheme Phase II. 28 March 2022.
Source: SIDBI.

Key Features and Challenges

Following are the **key features** of the list-based approach, designed to enhance scheme uptake, reduce transaction costs, and facilitate technology adoption in e-mobility and energy efficiency through innovative incentives:

(i) Increases the uptake of the schemes.
(ii) **Reduces transaction costs** by removing the need for energy studies and providing **interest subventions**.
(iii) **Removes the need for collateral and the equipment itself works as collateral** (under SPEED Plus, no immovable property is required).
(iv) **Promotes growth** in the adoption of new technologies in **e-mobility** and energy efficiency and productivity through incentives.

Key challenges of the list-based approach include:

(i)   It promotes only equipment-based (i.e., asset-based) financing of energy efficiency equipment, and has no emphasis on retrofitting and process improvement technologies.

(ii)   Technologies listed under the scheme are perceived as productivity and quality improvement technologies, which broadens the spectrum of the scheme. Many policymakers do not consider these schemes as pure energy efficiency projects.

(iii)   An ecosystem that is required to foster wider adoption of electric vehicle charging infrastructure is lacking.

Detailed observations of the schemes are presented in Appendix 6.

As a baseline study is not carried out, actual energy savings or impact cannot be measured.

Technical Assistance Schemes

Technical assistance (TA) programs are critical in sectors where market mechanisms are highly underdeveloped. TA programs and schemes help develop the capacities of stakeholders, create awareness, and help demonstrate feasibility through pilot projects. Overall, TA programs are essential for market transformation. Three TA programs (detailed in Table 12) were operationalized for creating a pipeline of energy efficiency projects and generating demand for energy efficiency in MSMEs. Details of these schemes are presented in Appendix 5.

The Deutsche Gesellschaft für Internationale Zusammenarbeit (GIZ) and BEE are supporting the TA for energy-intensive MSME sectors (steel, paper, textiles, glass, food, etc.). Under this program, the TA is extended to MSME sectors for developing a long-term (2030–2040) energy conservation road map, benchmark energy consumption level, technology compendium, etc.

These interventions support the development of the pipeline of energy efficiency, CSI, and renewable energy opportunities in the clusters which will require financing to support long-term implementation. IFC supported a study for the ECO-Cities project where a pipeline of over $9 million was created for energy efficiency and renewable energy projects in SME units.[31]

---

[31]   Government of India, Bureau of Energy Efficiency. n.d. *Partial Risk Guarantee Fund for Energy Efficiency (PRGFEE)*. New Delhi.

Table 12: Summary of Technical Assistance-Supported Schemes

Name of Technical Assistance Scheme	Duration	Key Features / Target Micro, Small, and Medium-Size Enterprises	Implementation Support	Energy Efficiency, Climate Smart Infrastructure, Renewable Energy
Promoting Market Transformation for Energy Efficiency in MSMEs, UNIDO, GEF	2010–Ongoing	Aggregated size $0.1 million–$0.25 million (Overall potential identified ~$25 million; 80,600 ton of emission reduction)	Yes	Energy efficiency
Promoting Energy Efficiency and Renewable Energy in Selected MSME Clusters in India[a]	2011–2022	5 energy-intensive sectors covering 23 clusters (EE Implementations in more than 800 MSME units)	Yes	Energy efficiency, renewable energy
Financing Energy Efficiency Programme	2015–Ongoing	Awareness programs (multiple seminars, webinar conducted). Grading energy efficiency projects (No uptake as of 2022), etc.	Pilot projects	Energy efficiency
Financing Energy Efficiency at MSMEs (FEEM) – WB – GEF (SIDBI, BEE)	2010–2019	Energy Audits and interest sub interventions (implementation of over $41 million was supported by TA under the project)	Yes	Energy efficiency, CSI, renewable energy

BEE = Bureau of Energy Efficiency; CSI = climate smart infrastructure; FEEM = Financing Energy Efficiency at MSMEs; GEF = Global Environment Facility; MSMEs = micro, small, and medium-sized enterprises; SIDBI = Small Industries Development Bank of India; TA = technical assistance; UNIDO = United Nations Industrial Development Organization, WB = World Bank.
Notes:
[a] BEE SME Project initiative.
[b] The scheme was withdrawn and details are presented on past programs on energy efficiency in Appendix 5.
Source: PWC's own research and consultation with stakeholders.

Key Features of the Technical Assistance Schemes

The technical assistance schemes exhibit notable strengths and areas for improvement in fostering energy efficiency within clusters. These include successful programmatic interventions that have cultivated an energy efficiency culture and facilitated significant investments, albeit with challenges such as limited outreach to targeted clusters and varying implementation rates among participants.

Pros

(i)   The programmatic interventions have resulted in the development of a culture for energy efficiency in clusters.

(ii) Support provided in these programs has resulted in an energy efficiency investment of over $200,000.

Con

Schemes have limited outreach to the focused clusters, and few clusters witness large implementations based on the peer-to-peer learning implementation rate in the cluster (units that are not front-runners and progressive take longer to implement energy efficiency technologies) and other clusters take longer lead times.

Understanding the Policy Landscape of India's Electric Vehicle Ecosystem

At the core of India's e-mobility ecosystem lies several carefully designed, intricate policies and regulatory frameworks that have been created by various ministries and regulatory bodies (Table 13).

Table 13: Details of Regulators Developing the Electric Vehicle Ecosystem

S. No.	Name of Regulatory Body	Role
1	Ministry of Heavy Industries and Public Enterprises	Under the Ministry of Heavy Industries and Public Enterprises, the Department of Heavy Industries has been looking after policy intervention and implementation to increase the adoption of electric vehicles in the country. The Department of Heavy Industries notified the FAME-I scheme in 2015 and FAME-II scheme in 2019 with a focus on four key areas in developing the electric vehicle ecosystem: technology development, demand incentives, charging infrastructure, and pilot projects.
2	Ministry of Road Transport and Highways	Under the Ministry of Road Transport and Highways, the Automotive Research Association of India is responsible for carrying out all research and engineering-related work. This serves as input for the ministry in developing incentives (especially nonfiscal) to promote electric vehicle adoption by consumers.
3	Ministry of Power	The Ministry of Power, through its Bureau of Energy Efficiency, and state nodal agencies are actively engaging to create policies and frameworks for creating a network of charging stations and infrastructure in the country.
4	Ministry of Housing and Urban Affairs	The Ministry of Housing and Urban Affairs has been responsible for engaging with residential and/or housing, as well as commercial public spaces, to create spaces for electric vehicle charging within their respective premises.
5	Ministry of Finance	The Ministry of Finance has been actively spearheading fiscal intervention in the e-mobility space through various measures such as income tax rebates, reduction in goods and services tax rates, etc.
6	Ministry of Environment, Forest and Climate Change	The Ministry of Environment, Forest and Climate Change has been an important stakeholder in India's National Electric Mobility Mission Plan (2020) initiative as well as in notifying the Draft Battery Waste Management Rules (2020).

FAME = Faster Adoption and Manufacturing of (Hybrid and) Electric Vehicles.
Sources: 1. Ministry of Heavy Industries. 30 November 2023. Home. New Delhi; 2. Ministry of Road Transport and Highways. 8 December 2023. About Us; 3. Ministry of Power. 7 December 2023. Home; 4. Ministry of Housing and Urban Affairs. 2017. Home; 5. Ministry of Finance. 17 November 2023. Home; 6. Ministry of Environment, Forest and Climate Change. 9 November 2023.

Figure 13 is a diagrammatic representation of India's timeline and progress in the e-mobility space during 2011–2022 through various national policies and initiatives.

The Faster Adoption and Manufacturing of (Hybrid and) Electric Vehicles (FAME) I and II policies have been at the forefront of India's e-mobility evolution. The two policies paved the way for creation of a road map for the implementation and execution of policies and measures in the electric vehicle landscape of the country.

The FAME initiative was first launched by the Department of Heavy Industries (DHI) in 2015 under the National Electric Mobility Mission.[32] This program aims to encourage the adoption of electric and hybrid vehicles by way of providing financial incentives and support. Phase one of the scheme (FAME-I) was initially implemented for 2 years (FY2015–2016 and FY2016–2017). It was extended for another year until FY2018–2019. This was followed by the launch of phase two of the scheme (FAME-II) from FY2019–2020 until FY2021–2022.

---

[32]   Government of India, Department of Heavy Industries. n.d. *FAME India Scheme Phase I*. New Delhi.

Figure 13: Timeline and Progress of E-mobility, 2011–2022

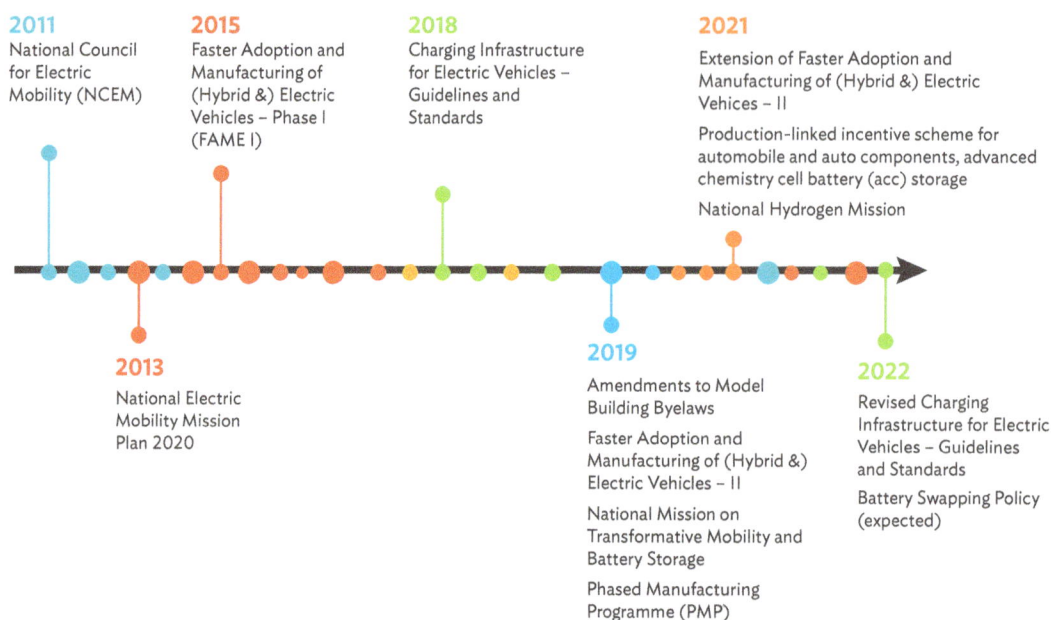

2011
National Council for Electric Mobility (NCEM)

2015
Faster Adoption and Manufacturing of (Hybrid &) Electric Vehicles – Phase I (FAME I)

2018
Charging Infrastructure for Electric Vehicles – Guidelines and Standards

2021
Extension of Faster Adoption and Manufacturing of (Hybrid &) Electric Vehices – II

Production-linked incentive scheme for automobile and auto components, advanced chemistry cell battery (acc) storage

National Hydrogen Mission

2013
National Electric Mobility Mission Plan 2020

2019
Amendments to Model Building Byelaws

Faster Adoption and Manufacturing of (Hybrid &) Electric Vehicles – II

National Mission on Transformative Mobility and Battery Storage

Phased Manufacturing Programme (PMP)

2022
Revised Charging Infrastructure for Electric Vehicles – Guidelines and Standards

Battery Swapping Policy (expected)

Source: PwC project experience.

The FAME-I scheme was launched with an overall outlay of ~$100 million. It was later extended with an additional outlay of $12.5 million. Under the FAME-I scheme, funds were allocated to provide direct subsidies to electric vehicle buyers. Although the scheme did not fully succeed in utilizing its allocated fund of $112.5 million, it was crucial for creating the required awareness and momentum in India's electric vehicle market. As part of the scheme, several pilot projects for electric vehicles were sanctioned along with the sanctioning of grants required for research and development, technology development, etc. in the electric vehicle ecosystem.

In March 2019, the FAME-II scheme was launched by the Ministry of Heavy Industries and Public Enterprises with an overall outlay of $1.25 billion including a spillover of $47 million from FAME-I. Some of the key modifications in FAME-II are as follows: [33]

(i)   The DHI increased the demand incentive for electric two-wheelers to ~$185/kWh from $125/kWh, while raising incentive caps to 40% of the cost of vehicles from 20%.

(ii)   EESL was appointed as the designated agency for aggregating demand for electric buses and electric three-wheelers.

---

[33]   Government of India, Department of Heavy Industries. n.d. FAME India Scheme Phase II. New Delhi.

Table 14: FAME I and FAME II Budget Outlay

Initial allocation of funds under FAME-I ($ million)				Initial allocation of funds under FAME-I ($ million)				
Component	2015–2016	2016–2017	Total Fund	Component	2019–2020	2020–2021	2021–2022	Total Fund
Technology Platform	8.8	15.0	23.8	Demand Incentives	102.8	573.4	398.4	1,074.5
Demand Incentive	19.4	42.5	61.9	Charging Infrastructure	37.5	50.0	37.5	125.0
Charging Infrastructure	1.3	2.5	3.8	Administrative Expenditure	1.5	1.6	1.6	4.8
Pilot Projects	2.5	6.3	8.8	Total for FAME-II	141.8	625.0	437.5	1,204.3
IEC / Operations	0.6	0.6	1.3	Committed from FAME-I	45.8	–	–	45.8
Total	32.5	66.9	99.4	Total	187.5	625.0	437.5	1,250.0

FAME = Faster Adoption and Manufacturing of (Hybrid and) Electric Vehicles; IEC = information, education and communication.
Source: Government of India, Ministry of Information and Broadcasting. 2022. Faster Adoption and Manufacturing of (Hybrid and) Electric Vehicles in India. Press release. July 11. New Delhi.

Policies Supporting Women Entrepreneurship

There has been a lower representation of women-led businesses, especially in the industrial sectors. However, with the different evolving new tech businesses and services in the country, the role of women has been increasing in the SME sectors (especially in commercial buildings and e-mobility). Manufacturing services in India have been traditionally male-driven, but women's participation in different roles has been increasing (especially in technology and CSI). It is imperative to foster these technologies through policy, financial subsidies, and regulations to improve gender parity.

The Government of India is undertaking initiatives in the form of policy intervention to strengthen women-led entrepreneurs in the country and promote entrepreneurship at the micro and small enterprise level through multiple programmatic interventions.

In 2013, a women-only bank—**Bhartiya Mahila Bank**—was launched to cater to the various banking needs of women. The bank's products and services were designed to provide concessions to women borrowers on loan interest rates.

(i) In 2015, the **Pradhan Mantri Mudra Yojana** was launched and aimed at providing collateral-free loans of up to $12,500 for micro and small enterprises.[34] As per data shared by the Ministry of Finance in 2021, close to **70% of the loans were disbursed to women entrepreneurs**.

(ii) There has also been significant improvement in providing women access to bank accounts, primarily driven due to the introduction of the government policy **Pradhan Mantri Jan Dhan Yojana**. As per the All-India Debt and Investment Survey (2019), around 80.7% of women in rural areas and 81.3% of women in urban areas had deposits in their bank accounts.[35]

---

[34] Mudra.n.d. *Pradhan Mantri Mudra Yojana*. Mumbai.
[35] Government of India, Ministry of Finance. 2020. *Economic Survey 2019-20*. New Delhi.

(iii) In 2016, **Stand Up India** was launched by the Government of India to offer loans ranging from $12,500 to $125,000 for the underserved segments of society such as **women-led businesses**, businesses led by other groups, etc.[36] **More than 81% of the loans sanctioned under Stand-Up India were disbursed to women entrepreneurs**.

(iv) In 2018, NITI Aayog set up a **Women Entrepreneurship Platform** to provide support to emerging and existing women entrepreneurs across the country, through free credit ratings, mentorship, funding support, apprenticeship, and corporate partnerships.[37]

Observations on Financing Schemes

A summary of the key takeaways from the different schemes and programs is presented in Table 15.

Table 15: Summary of Key Financing Schemes and Takeaways

Major Feature	Key Schemes	Observations	Takeaways
Risk guarantee mechanism	PRSF **Low uptake**	• Reorient the lender perspective from collateral-based lending to project financing • ESCO ecosystem is not available as required for the scalability of the scheme • Lack of incentives and regulations for ESPC contracting and M&V protocols	Risk guarantee schemes help in de-linking the risk of the projected energy performance and can be used for developing financing solutions for state-of-the-art technologies and highly customizable technologies. Lower risk premiums with flexibility in norms in existing risk guarantee schemes will help in larger adoption.
	USAID DFC guarantee scheme for solar photovoltaics	• Portfolio-based risk guarantee increases flexibility in coverage for individual loan cases • Dynamic policy and regulatory frameworks in different states make renewable energy investment highly sensitive	
	CGTMSE **High uptake**	• Simple procedural norms, hence higher uptake, supported by MoMSME	
List-based scheme	SIDBI SPEED Plus SIDBI, Star **Medium uptake**	• Pre-approved list of technologies helps in faster loan appraisal, hence higher uptake • SPEED Plus scheme promotes collaboration with OEMs and vendors • Mainly focuses on asset financing of equipment, with no emphasis on retrofitting	Commercial technologies can be promoted through list-based approach with innovative financing instruments.

continued on next page

---

[36] Small Industries Development Bank. n.d. *Stand Up India Scheme*.
[37] Government of India, NITI Aayog. 2021. *The Women Entrepreneurship Platform*.

Table 15 *continued*

Major Feature	Key Schemes	Observations	Takeaways
Subsidy schemes	CLCSS and TUFS **High uptake**	• High uptake of the scheme due to direct financial benefits through ministry for technology upgrades • Widely disseminated through a comprehensive list of lending institutes • Presently this scheme is being revamped	Technologies that have a higher payback and possess higher GHG reduction potential should be supported through subsidies along with thrust for reducing the cost through economies of scale (e.g., LED lights)
	FAME – I and FAME II **Low uptake**	• Challenges in the life of battery and reliability compared to internal combustion engines, lower battery range • Lesser penetration of electric vehicle charging infrastructure across cities	
Revolving funds for EE	SIDBI 4E Scheme **Medium uptake** EESL GEF **Low uptake**	• Requires pipeline generation at cluster or sector level for faster uptake • Benefits such as interest subsidies or lower costs are required for uptake • Scheme requirements for energy study at each loan case increases the lead time for the 4E scheme	Success of the scheme has led to the rollout of similar schemes from SIDBI. Interest subsidies help in improving the payback and should be included for the technologies with higher GHG reduction potential.

4E = end to end energy efficiency; CGTMSE = Credit Guarantee Scheme for Micro and Small Enterprises; CLCSS = Credit Linked Capital Subsidy Scheme; DFC = Development Finance Corporation; EESL = Energy Efficiency Services Limited; ESCO = energy service company; ESPC = energy saving performance contract; FAME = Faster Adoption and Manufacturing of (Hybrid and) Electric Vehicles; GEF = Global Environment Facility; GHG = greenhouse gas; LED = light emitting diode; M&V = measurement and verification; MoMSME = Ministry of Micro, Small and Medium Enterprises; OEM = original equipment manufacturer; PRSF = partial risk sharing facility; SIDBI = Small Industries Development Bank of India; TUFS = Technology Upgradation Funding Scheme; USAID = United States Agency for International Development.

Source: PwC project experience.

6 STRENGTHS, WEAKNESSES, OPPORTUNITIES, AND THREATS ANALYSIS AND POLICY RECOMMENDATIONS

Strengths, Weaknesses, Opportunities, and Threats Analysis and Understanding the Opportunities in Energy Efficiency and Climate-Smart Infrastructure

This chapter attempts to identify the strengths, weaknesses, opportunities, and threats (SWOT) in the financing ecosystem which can be leveraged by NBFCs and financial institutions through the support of the international development agencies and strategic planning processes for long-term decarbonization. The study carried out a SWOT analysis on the energy efficiency and CSI financing ecosystem of SMEs based on desk research and multiple consultations with different stakeholders (Figure 14).

Figure 14: Strengths, Weaknesses, Opportunities, and Threats Analysis of the Energy Efficiency and Climate-Smart Infrastructure Financing Ecosystem

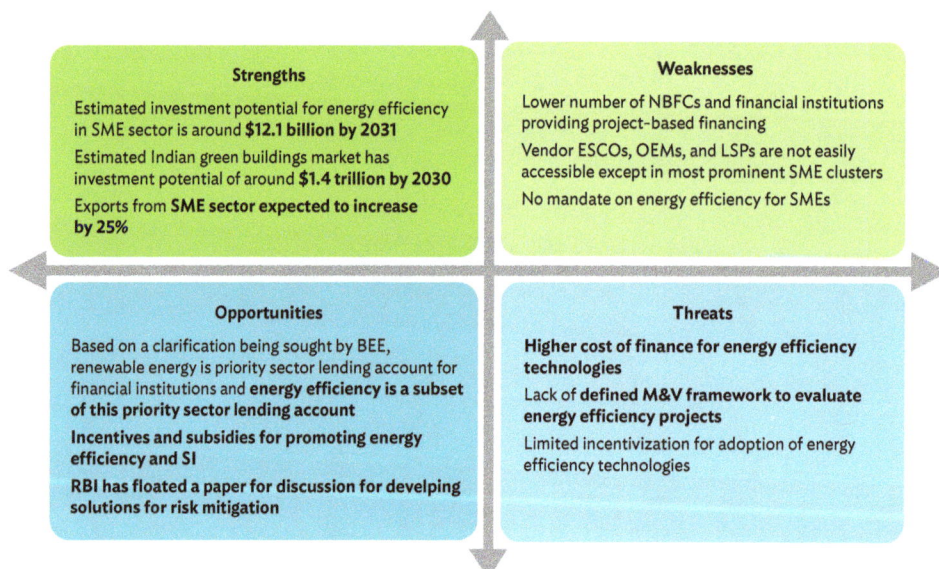

Strengths

Estimated investment potential for energy efficiency in SME sector is around **$12.1 billion by 2031**

Estimated Indian green buildings market has investment potential of around **$1.4 trillion by 2030**

Exports from **SME sector expected to increase by 25%**

Weaknesses

Lower number of NBFCs and financial institutions providing project-based financing

Vendor ESCOs, OEMs, and LSPs are not easily accessible except in most prominent SME clusters

No mandate on energy efficiency for SMEs

Opportunities

Based on a clarification being sought by BEE, renewable energy is priority sector lending account for financial institutions and **energy efficiency is a subset of this priority sector lending account**

Incentives and subsidies for promoting energy efficiency and SI

RBI has floated a paper for discussion for develping solutions for risk mitigation

Threats

Higher cost of finance for energy efficiency technologies

Lack of **defined M&V framework to evaluate energy efficiency projects**

Limited incentivization for adoption of energy efficiency technologies

BEE = Bureau of Energy Efficiency, ESCO = energy service company, LSP = local service provider, M&V = measurement and verification, NBFC = nonbanking financial company, OEM = original equipment manufacturer, RBI = Reserve Bank on India, SI = smart infrastructure, SMEs = small and medium-sized enterprises.
Sources: Government of India, Bureau of Energy Efficiency. 2019. Strategy Plan Towards Developing an Energy Efficient Nation (2017-2031). New Delhi; Government of India, Bureau of Energy Efficiency; Multiple International Finance Corporation. Climate Investment Opportunities in South Asia; Reserve Bank of India. n.d. Discussion Paper on Climate Risk and Sustainable Finance; and discussions with key stakeholders.

An environment scan and SWOT analysis identified several opportunities and challenges. These can be addressed through policy push and programmatic interventions for this sector, such as:

(i) Developing a long-term mandate on energy efficiency through the strengthening of the Energy Conservation Building Code for commercial buildings, the launch of Perform Achieve and Earn for SMEs, and mandating the energy audits in medium- to large-scale units.[38]

(ii) Strengthening the development of the state-of-the-art manufacturing facilities through incentives in the form of production-linked incentive (PLI) schemes to reduce the import challenges. The production linked incentivization scheme has been institutionalized for developing technologies for electric vehicles, batteries, and renewable energy, which will resolve risks in the long run. The government can extend this scheme to other key sectors.

(iii) Developing economies of scale for state-of-the-art technologies by promoting research and development, developing centers of excellence, and demand aggregation. EESL has been working with different stakeholders (Global Environment Facility [GEF] and United Nations Industrial Development Organization [UNIDO]) for standardization and promoting economies of scale for energy efficiency technologies.

(iv) **Support can be provided through blended finance, risk-sharing facility for asset-based financing. This will strengthen the energy efficiency financing ecosystem.**

(v) While BEE has been working from time to time on the development of the ESCO ecosystem, there is still a significant need for creating enabling policies—including fiscal and taxation-related incentives— for the ESCO model, creation of standard templates for ESCO performance contracts, M&V guidelines for ESCOs, etc. This will help to reduce the scope for ambiguities inherent in ESCO implementations at SMEs and in the related energy efficiency financing framework.

(vi) **The Government of India is planning to include energy efficiency under priority sector lending**, which will further help different players access the funds.

The pledge to install 500 gigawatts of renewable energy power by 2030 will help in drastically reducing long-term carbon emissions from different economic sectors.[39] These initiatives will help resolve the risks associated with long-term decarbonization goals. Energy efficiency and CSI are being prioritized by the government to achieve long-term decarbonization goals.

To develop a complete ecosystem, policy and regulatory factors will play a significant role. These interventions can be facilitated through government policymakers and regulators as well as supported by multilateral and bilateral development agencies. Several of these are being actively considered and driven by the government:

(i) Systemic policy support helps both end consumers and technology providers. This could include mandating the minimum energy standards for the equipment and facilitating financing through developing priority sector lending accounts.

(ii) Investments that support domestic manufacturing of energy efficiency technology solutions, CSI, allied solutions, etc. This includes better access to consumer finance, an extension of the PLI scheme for energy efficiency equipment.

(iii) Developing new and innovative business models that thrive on public–private alliances and partnerships through the strengthening of risk guarantee mechanism and standardization of an M&V framework.

---

[38] Perform Achieve and Earn is a voluntary scheme envisaged by BEE for the SME industries. Participating SMEs will be given specific energy reduction targets and overachievers will be incentivized. The scheme is envisaged on similar lines to the policy mandated and market-based scheme Perform Achieve and Trade which is being implemented by BEE with encouraging outcomes for large industries.

[39] Government of India, Ministry of Power. 2021. Mission 500 GW by 2030. Press release. 16 November. New Delhi.

(iv)   Policy action to bring energy efficiency into the ambit of priority sector lending.[40]

(v)   Developing research and development facilities for progress in the new age technologies and providing commercialized solutions.

Strengths, Weaknesses, Opportunities, and Threats Analysis and Understanding the Opportunities in E-mobility Financing

The study carried out a SWOT analysis of the e-mobility financing ecosystem of SMEs based on desk research and multiple consultations with different stakeholders (Figure 15).

Figure 15: Strengths, Weaknesses, Opportunities, and Threats Analysis of the E-mobility Financing Ecosystem

Strengths

Active policy intervention by both central and state governments through several fiscal incentives to promote the adoption of electric vehicles

Production-Linked Incentive scheme worth ₹ **181 billion** approved investments in electric vehicle battery manufacturing

100% **fleet electrification** commitment by leading players such as Amazon, Capgemini, Zomato, etc. by 2030–2040

Venture funding of **$601 million** raised by several start-ups in the Indian electric vehicle landscape in FY2019

Weaknesses

Inadequate charging infrastructure and the consequent range anxiety

Dependency on the People's Republic of China, the Republic of Korea, and other countries for the import of batteries, components, and parts

High up-front prices

Lack of options for **high-performance electric vehicles**

Inadequate maintenance and repair facilities

Opportunities

NITI Aayog and World Bank are in the process of setting up a **$300 million** risk-sharing instrument that will act as a **guarantee mechanism** for banks and NBFCs in case of payment delay or default on electric vehicle loans

NITI Aayog has also proposed the central bank of India, i.e., RBI to include electric vehicles in its **priority-sector lending** guidelines as it presents the opportunity for banks and NBFCs to achieve electric vehicle financing market size of ₹40.0 billion by 2025

Threats

Potential global **shortage of lithium** and cobalt by 2025

To make electric vehicles truly a green option, they need to be powered by electricity that is generated through **renewable sources** of energy such as solar, wind, etc. and not rely on coal-powered electricity

Fire-related accidents of two-wheeler electric vehicles in India have been a major deterrent to customer confidence in electric vehicles

$ = United States dollars, ₹ = Indian rupee, FY = fiscal year, NBFC = nonbanking financial company, RBI = Reserve Bank of India.

Sources: Government of India, NITI Aayog and Deutsche Gesellschaft für Internationale Zusammenarbeit. 2021. Status Quo Analysis of Various Segments of Electric Mobility and Low Carbon Passenger Road Transport in India. New Delhi; Government of India, Bureau of Energy Efficiency. 2019. Strategy Plan Towards Developing an Energy Efficient Nation (2017–2031). Delhi; Government of India, Department of Heavy Industries. 2022. PLI Scheme for National Programme on Advanced Chemistry Cell (ACC) Battery Storage. New Delhi; Reserve Bank of India. n.d. Discussion Paper on Climate Risk and Sustainable Finance; Government of India, https://www.niti.gov. in/sites/default/files/2021-; NITI Aayog and Rocky Mountain Institute. 2021. Mobilising Finance for EVs in India; World Business Council for Sustainable Development. 2019. India Business Guide to EV Adoption; Government of India, NITI Aayog, RMI, and RMI India. 2022. Banking on Electric Vehicles in India: A Blueprint for Inclusion of EVs in Priority Sector Lending Guidelines; Government of India, Press Information Bureau. 2022. NITI Aayog, Rocky Mountain Institute (RMI), and RMI India release the 'Banking on Electric Vehicles in India' report. Press release. New Delhi; World Economic Forum. 2022. The world needs 2 billion electric vehicles to get to net zero. But is there enough lithium to make all the batteries?; and multiple discussions with key stakeholders.

---

[40]   Priority sector lending is the role exercised by the RBI to banks, imploring them to dedicate funds for specific sectors of the economy like renewable energy, agriculture, and allied activities, education, and housing and food for the poorer population.

An environment scan and SWOT analysis identified several opportunities and challenges. These can be addressed through policy push and programmatic interventions for this sector, such as:

(i)   Strengthening the development of the state-of-the-art manufacturing facilities through incentives in the form of a PLI scheme to reduce the import challenges. The PLI scheme has been institutionalized for developing battery renewable energy technologies, which will resolve the risks in the long run. The government can extend this scheme for other key sectors like electric vehicles in the longer term (i.e., beyond the horizon of the subsidies under the FAME scheme).

(ii)   NITI Aayog is progressively developing an ecosystem to support e-mobility as a sunrise sector, which will give a boost to economic growth and employment potential. NITI Aayog is supporting collaboration between the government and DFIs for devising innovative risk mitigation instruments that can address the major challenges associated with the wider adoption of e-mobility, including ease of access to e-mobility finance.

(iii)   A battery swapping policy was announced in the budget as a key area of focus during the budget speech from the finance minister in 2022.[41] This will help address the technology and operational risks associated with storage batteries in the e-mobility space and in developing a conducive environment to foster financing in the sector.

(iv)   The Government of India is also planning to include e-mobility under priority sector lending, which will further help different players access finance.

(v)   Battery management rules and electric vehicle policies have been supported by the states in the recent past. Many states have announced an electric vehicle policy and some states have also incorporated incentivization for extended battery warranty programs, better buyback programs from OEMs, etc. These policy-driven initiatives and the involvement of OEMs will help address key risk areas associated with e-mobility.

(vi)   Considering the potential shortage of lithium for electric vehicle batteries, developing and evolving technology for new metal-based batteries and recycling old batteries will help to overcome the potential barrier.

There are significant opportunities in the e-mobility market space given the focus of the government and international development agencies community on long-term initiatives planned to eliminate the associated risks. The private sector—with well-considered and planned interventions—can leverage the significant financing opportunities in this market space and develop or expand their financing portfolios in this sector, while helping to achieve India's long-term decarbonization goals. It is imperative to understand the barriers and challenges faced by the different stakeholders and develop financing solutions that can enhance the uptake of energy efficiency, CSI, and e-mobility.

---

[41]   Government of India, Public Information Bureau. 2022. Union Minister for Finance and Corporate Affairs announces the proposal for bringing out Battery Swapping Policy and inter-operability standards. Press release. 1 February.

7 BARRIERS AND OPPORTUNITIES IN FINANCING ENERGY EFFICIENCY, CLIMATE-SMART INFRASTRUCTURE, AND E-MOBILITY

Mapping Private Sector Financial Institutions and Nonbanking Financial Companies Working in the Small and Medium-Sized Enterprise Segment

Financial institutions play an important role in developing the energy efficiency, CSI, and e-mobility market in India. Even with the opportunity of a new line of business and significant investment potential, energy efficiency, CSI, and e-mobility remain only on the periphery of their focus.

To understand the perspective of the financial institutions in terms of the opportunities and challenges of leveraging energy efficiency, CSI, and e-mobility investment potential, stakeholders have been mapped into three categories: private banks, NBFCs, and financial technology (fintech) companies.

The study found key insights from financial institutions concerning energy efficiency and SME financing and the challenges faced in these sectors. The short-listed financial institutions are presented in Table 16, and the methodology adopted for the selection is in Appendix 3.

Table 16: Short-Listed Financial Institutions and Nonbanking Financial Companies

Name	Type	Empanelment and/or Key Lending Accounts
Akasa Financial Services	NBFC	Electric mobility, SME loans
Axis Bank	FI	Sustainable lending
Caspian Impact Investments	NBFC	Clean energy, energy efficiency
Ckers Finance	NBFC	Clean energy, Resource efficiency
Edelweiss Financial Services	NBFC	Clean energy and SME lending
Electronica Finance	NBFC	Energy efficiency in MSME, rooftop solar, climate finance
Federal Bank	FI	Energy efficiency, sustainable lending
HSBC Bank	FI	ESCO financing and demand-side management initiatives
ICICI Bank Limited	FI	Energy efficiency, sustainable financing (renewable energy)
IDFC First Bank	FI	PRSF/PRGFEE
IndoStar Capital Finance Limited	NBFC	Commercial vehicle and electric mobility
IndusInd Bank	FI	PRSF/PRGFEE
Investment and Finance Company Ltd.	NBFC	Commercial vehicle and electric mobility

continued on next page

Table 16 *continued*

Name	Type	Empanelment and/or Key Lending Accounts
IREDA	NBFC	Renewable energy, energy efficiency
Kotak Mahindra Bank	FI	Energy efficiency, renewable purchase obligation
L&T Infrastructure Finance	NBFC	Solar and wind energy projects
Northern Arc	NBFC	Electric mobility
PTC Financial Services Limited	FI	PRSF/PRGFEE
Rev Fin	FinTech	Electric mobility
Siemens Financial Services	NBFC	Energy transition, leasing
TATA Cleantech	NBFC	CleanTech solutions, sustainable strategy
Yes Bank	FI	ESCO financing / PRGFEE / PRSF

CleanTech = Clean Technology; ESCO = energy service company; FI = financial institution; Fintech = financial technology; IREDA = Indian Renewable Energy Development Agency Limited; MSME = micro, small, and medium-sized enterprises; NBFC = nonbanking financial company; PRGFEE = Partial Risk Guarantee Fund for Energy Efficiency; PRSF = partial risk sharing facility; SME = small and medium-sized enterprises.
Source: Primary consultations.

Throughout the study, several instances emerged where NBFCs stood out in terms of their understanding of the domain, effort, and collaborative relationships with stakeholders in the value chain (like ESCOs, vendor ESCOs, and technology suppliers). They could leverage their market strengths and demand aggregation capabilities and had an overall willingness to adapt to the demands of the energy efficiency, CSI, and e-mobility financing domain.

Considering that several NBFCs are well-positioned for leveraging their strengths aligned with the energy efficiency, CSI, and e-mobility financing space, weightage and special attention were given to NBFCs during the identification of financial institutions and the short-listing for consultations. Details of the expertise of NBFCs and financial institutions consulted during the project are in Table 17.[42]

Table 17: Expertise Supporting Clean Energy Financing

Name	Type	Expertise in Evaluating Energy Efficiency Projects	Expertise in Leasing Models	Financing E-mobility	ESCO / RESCO Financing	MSME Loans	Empaneled under Risk Guarantee Schemes
Akasa Finance Ltd	NBFC			✓		✓	
Axis Bank*	FI					✓	
Caspian Impact Investment	NBFC	✓			✓	✓	
cKers Finance	NBFC	✓	✓	✓	✓	✓	
Edelweiss Financial Services*	NBFC					✓	

continued on next page

---

[42] The broader objective of this review is to explore the different financing models relevant to energy efficiency and CSI that are prevalent in the market and some of the financial institutions supporting these models. This is not intended to be a comprehensive list of the capabilities of financial institutions.

Table 17 *continued*

Name	Type	Expertise in Evaluating Energy Efficiency Projects	Expertise in Leasing Models	Financing E-mobility	ESCO / RESCO Financing	MSME Loans	Empaneled under Risk Guarantee Schemes
Electronica Finance Limited	NBFC	✓	✓		✓	✓	✓
Federal Bank	FI					✓	✓
HSBC Bank*	FI	✓				✓	
ICICI Bank Limited*	FI					✓	
IDFC First Bank*	FI					✓	✓
IndoStar Capital Finance Limited*	NBFC			✓		✓	
IndusInd Bank*	FI					✓	✓
Investment and Finance Company Ltd.*	NBFC			✓		✓	
IREDA	NBFC	✓		✓	✓	✓	
Kotak Mahindra Bank*	FI					✓	
L&T Infrastructure Finance*	NBFC						
Northern Arc Capital	NBFC			✓		✓	
PTC Financial Services Limited*	NBFC	✓					✓
RevFin	Fintech			✓			
Siemens Financial	NBFC	✓	✓			✓	
Tata Cleantech Capital Limited	NBFC	✓			✓	✓	✓
YES Bank	FI			✓		✓	✓

ESCO = energy service company; FI = financial institution; IREDA = Indian Renewable Energy Development Agency Limited; MSME = micro, small, and medium-sized enterprises; NBFC = nonbanking financial company; RESCO = renewable energy service company.

* Not consulted for this report. Evaluation is based on secondary research only (with a focus on the major business initiatives presented by these firms in the public domain).

Source: Primary consultations.

Challenges and Barriers to the Financing of Energy Efficiency and Climate-Smart Infrastructure

The discussion guide adopted for primary consultations with technology providers for this report is in Appendix 7, and the discussion guide for financing institutions is in Appendix 8.

Challenges and Barriers to Financing Energy Efficiency and Climate-Smart Infrastructure Solutions

(i) **The average ticket size of energy efficiency and CSI loans generally ranges from a few hundred dollars to over $125,000. Financial institutions and NBFCs are typically interested in lending for higher ticket sizes.** The minimum ticket size that financial institutions and NBFCs prefer for lending lies in the range of $62,500–$625,000. OEMs and LSPs face challenges during the sale of energy efficiency equipment as SMEs are not able to get access to finance for lower ticket sizes.

(ii) **Financial institutions and NBFCs charge interest premiums while lending to SMEs.** This increases the interest rates, but the financiers are also *partially financing the assets with an overall lower than market loan-to-value ratio*. Higher interest rates hinder the larger uptake of energy efficiency and CSI projects with medium to higher payback periods as these rates inflate the financial payback and drop the internal rate of return (IRR) and net present value for the projects. Higher interest rates also decreased the viability of the ESCO-based projects and sales of capital-intensive energy efficiency and CSI equipment financing.

(iii) **A few financial institutions have been associated with risk-sharing schemes** such as SIDBI's partial risk sharing facility (PRSF); however, there has been limited or nil participation and/or utilization of these mechanisms. The ticket size of projects associated with such schemes is generally on the lower side. ESCOs face challenges to avail the project-based financing for the implantation of energy efficiency and CSI ESCO projects. Most ESCOs in India are smaller and have a debt skewed balance sheet and, in the absence of project financing, they are not able to execute larger ESCO projects.

(iv) Several **financial institutions have expressed their inability to understand the technicalities** of energy savings or energy efficiency-related projects that are usually undertaken by ESCOs. While energy savings-related projects contribute to the bottom line of the company, they rarely affect the top-line, i.e., the revenues of the company. As a result of their inability to generate any tangible production-related cash outflow, most financiers find it difficult to understand how energy savings can be captured as actual cash flow savings to ensure their repayment security.

(v) **Only a handful of financial institutions provide asset-based financing solutions.** These financial solutions are limited to a handful of the standard technologies (e.g., plastic manufacturing—molding and injection machines—done by few NBFCs). There is no risk coverage or any other support offered under any program to these financial institutions in case of default. In case of a loan default, the financier has the option to recover the loan amount by seizing the physical asset. *Only limited OEMs and LSPs can serve SME units under an asset-based financing model.*

(vi) **Most financial institutions have dedicated financial products that cater to the MSME segment for working capital loans, term loans, and business loans.** However, the majority of the leading **financial institutions do not have specialized financial schemes or products that are dedicated to the clean energy financing segments:** energy efficiency projects or equipment financing.

Understanding the Barriers Faced by Women-Led Enterprises

Women-led enterprises face various barriers while accessing finance to grow their businesses:

(i) **Lack of collateral.** Women, who have traditionally been excluded from property ownership and land ownership, often fail to provide any collateral while availing loans from banks and financial institutions.

(ii) **Inherent biases and perceptions.** Women-led businesses are perceived to be high risk–low return in nature by financial institutions. Irrespective of whether the perceived high risk is based on facts or experiences or pure conjecture, it limits women-led businesses to access secure financing. When banks conduct their risk assessment of the loan applicants, female applicants are often asked to be accompanied by a male guarantor: a husband, brother, father, or any other male in the family.

(iii) **Lack of customized loan products.** Several financial institutions—including banks and NBFCs—do not have specific loan products that are designed specially to cater to women-led businesses. In the absence of a strong credit history and any substantial collateral, women struggle with generic loan products and services. Factors such as low loan repayment periods and high interest rates further reduce their chances of securing loans.

(iv) **Legal and compliance-related barriers.** In many cases, women belonging to rural or semi-urban areas also face compliance-related challenges while applying for a loan. Some women fail to provide legal documents that serve as prerequisites for a loan such as a national identity document, passport, etc.

Proposed Solutions for Strengthening Energy Efficiency and Climate-Smart Infrastructure Financing

During detailed consultations with private sector financial institutions, the study validated probable solutions that can foster energy efficiency financing through collaborative efforts of the institutes working in policy circles, international development agencies, and players working in the ecosystem. Several financial institutions expressed their concerns related to their overall low confidence in customized energy savings projects. To tackle this and to further mobilize investments in the domain of energy efficiency, technical assistance can be provided to financial institutions for developing financial products that are aligned toward the standardization and structuring of M&V and ESCO contracts, developing the case studies of successful implementations, and financing highly customized energy efficiency projects.

Facilitating Demand Aggregation Through Collaboration Between Financial Institutions and Technology Providers

Financial institutions have been trying to tackle the issue of the limited ticket size of energy efficiency projects. This calls for the bundling of projects or demand aggregation for financing. Some financial institutions consulted also expressed their concerns regarding the limited deal pipeline (i.e., limited demand among SMEs or project hosts) for energy efficiency and ESCO-related projects. The creation of deal pipelines through demand aggregation is a resource-intensive activity and involves significant customer acquisition costs.

ESCOs working in the country can carry out the bundling of projects as they are working with multiple SMEs, e.g., waste heat recovery solutions can cost from a few hundred to thousands of dollars, which is a lower ticket size for any financial institution or NBFC to finance. ESCOs can club the demand from different locations, SMEs, and clusters to formulate higher-value tickets in the range of $50,000–$100,000, which NBFCs can consider as one loan (ESCOs will do the publicity and provide the units with financed equipment and with performance guarantee).

The financial institution or NBFC will deal with one ESCO and provide the loan based on the energy savings projects and its credibility in the energy efficiency space. This will help in building the finances through collaborative efforts.

As a possible work-around to this problem, NBFCs and financial institutions can collaborate with ESCOs and OEMs to leverage their marketing channels for the aggregation of demand. NBFCs can standardize the technology financing and implementation solutions through collaborative efforts with ESCOs and OEMs to facilitate faster and more economical financing solutions.

Financial institutions, OEMs, and ESCOs—through long-term financing agreements and collaborative efforts—can solve this challenge of demand aggregation. Another possible solution can be through the development of integrated digital platforms that can help aggregate this demand.

Enabling Financial Institutions Through Portfolio-based Lines of Credit Coupled with Blended Finance

ESCOs—players who usually have medium- to small-scale operations—generally have to avail finance at a relatively higher cost from NBFCs and financial institutions. This impacts the financial viability and/or attractiveness of the project developed by them.

NBFCs are sometimes better placed for energy efficiency and CSI financing based on their existing portfolio, exposure to the sector dynamics, ability to evaluate the energy efficiency and CSI projects, etc. However, their typically higher cost of finance becomes a deterrent. This can be mitigated to an extent with blended finance.

Blended finance for energy efficiency will help lower the cost of finance, supporting a higher IRR for the energy efficiency and CSI project.

Long-term portfolio-based line of credit offerings from international development agencies, NBFCs, and financial institutions can especially be of relevance in this context. NBFCs can pass on the benefits of lower interest rates to the relevant stakeholders in the financing ecosystem, improving the viability and/or attractiveness of the projects and potentially improving the demand. NBFCs should ideally retain the flexibility to decide on interest rates based on the specific risk profiles of individual loan cases.

The line of credit can be provided by NBFCs or financial institutions to ESCOs or vendor ESCOs (small-scale OEMs) and service providers, where their business model involves financing the technology or equipment. This can be one of the ways for financial institutions to collaborate with technology providers and leverage their demand aggregation potential.

Portfolio-based Risk-Sharing Facilities

The single dedicated risk sharing facility for energy efficiency that is functional in the country is PRSF. PRSF has helped in supporting the ESCO project financing space, despite modest uptake due to various limiting factors including an underdeveloped ESCO ecosystem in the country. However, PRSF evaluates and offers risk coverage on a per project basis. *Portfolio-based risk guarantee mechanisms*, where risk cover is offered to financial institutions and NBFCs over their entire portfolio of energy efficiency, CSI, and e-mobility projects, have some distinct advantages.

These solutions offer financial institutions flexibility to provide varying degrees of coverage based on their risk assessment on individual projects. This **helps to optimize the guaranteed fee component by providing need-based coverage**.

Some of the smaller NBFCs with proven capacities to undertake project-based financing are not eligible for PRSF, limiting its reach. **Risk guarantee mechanisms** (preferably portfolio-based) that are agnostic to business models will help to expand coverage across the entire spectrum of energy efficiency and CSI projects irrespective of ESCO or other business models. Simplicity and user-friendly processes, coupled with moderate guaranteed fees, are critical to their success.

There is **limited availability of asset-based energy efficiency or CSI financing solutions to SMEs**. SMEs have to settle for collateral-based finance in many cases. This limits the faster adoption and penetration of the new energy efficiency and CSI technologies. Only a few NBFCs thrive predominantly on asset-based financing solutions, and that too for a limited set of technologies. Based on feedback from NBFCs, it was concluded that setting up a **risk guarantee fund for the asset-based financing** will help to expand the range of energy efficiency and CSI technologies covered through this financing model that has been proven to be user-friendly and scalable.

Technical Assistance for Energy Efficiency and Climate-Smart Infrastructure Financing

During consultations, financial institutions showed a limited understanding of energy efficiency and CSI projects. Some of the typical challenges faced by financial institutions are the absence of **standardization including standard contracts, frameworks, and tools** to evaluate energy savings and resultant cash flows; difficulties in **developing deal pipelines** given the limited demand from project hosts coupled with low ticket sizes; and inherent complexities associated with evaluation and financing of innovative or unfamiliar energy efficiency and CSI technologies, etc.

NBFCs and financial institutions have advocated the need for projects related to the financing of energy efficiency and CSI solutions. TA projects can assist financial institutions newly venturing into energy efficiency and CSI financing to address the various challenges.

In the case of asset financing, a TA project will help to standardize the financing solutions related to specific energy efficiency and CSI technologies. A **TA project for developing the standardization of the appraisal process for specific technologies and/or equipment** will support financial institutions and NBFCs with a better understanding to evaluate the cash flows, secondary market assessment, risk associated during the operations, and allied contingencies. A two-pronged approach that combines the TA with portfolio-based risk guarantees can support the uptake of assets-based financing solutions for SMEs.

Special Financing Schemes for Women

There is a need to create specialized loan products and services that treat women borrowers as a special category: **providing customized loan offerings to women-only businesses that suit their requirements**.

To address the large financing gap, **banks and NBFCs that are at the forefront of India's formal lending mechanism must earmark funds for women-owned enterprises**. This will encourage participation from more women-owned businesses in a space that has predominantly been male-dominated.

Women, who are often not able to provide any collateral, face higher chances of rejection of their loan applications. To remove this barrier, it would be helpful if **financial institutions allow women to provide any movable assets available to them as collateral**. For example, in many countries—while sanctioning loans to women—gold jewelry is accepted as collateral. **Alternative collateral, such as postdated checks or movable assets or business assets, must be explored while sanctioning loans to women-led businesses**.

Existing schemes by financial institutions for women entrepreneurs are presented in Appendix 6.

Challenges Associated with Electric Vehicle Financing in Micro, Small, and Medium-Sized Enterprises and Proposed Solutions for Strengthening the E-mobility Ecosystem

Despite many constant developments in the e-mobility ecosystem of India, several challenges and barriers stand in the way of electric vehicle adoption. Based on broad observations and detailed conversations with financial institutions, the following challenges and their possible solutions can help accelerate e-mobility financing in India:

(i) **Product-specific challenges.** A major barrier to electric vehicle adoption is its higher up-front cost compared to traditional ICE counterparts. While the central government and several state governments have been trying to bring down the costs through several incentives, such as goods and services tax rate cuts, lower vehicle registration costs, the cost of procuring an electric vehicle is still 1.2 to 3 times more than its counterpart ICE vehicle.

To tackle this, easy access to finance will be one of the most critical factors. However, without a strong proven performance track record, electric vehicle financing is not well accepted by financiers, both from the point of view of vehicle operation and maintenance as well as battery performance. In addition to this, the lack of a strong secondary market for electric vehicles acts as a major deterrent to the free flow of finance into the electric vehicle ecosystem.

Being a new age technology, financing institutions such as banks and NBFCs are not actively looking to lend for electric vehicles due to the inherent asset and business model-related risks. Since the broader market perception is that electric vehicles are not yet a proven vehicle type, their longevity and asset life remain questionable. Another challenge in the context of electric vehicles is the uncertainty about the price fluctuation related to electric vehicle batteries. This, coupled with apprehensions about the overall low battery life, is one of the major deterrents to electric vehicle financing.

Some of the financial institutions in the study are offering loans to electric vehicle OEMs or battery manufacturers for very low loan tenures, i.e., around 30 months. A shorter loan tenure automatically means an increase in equated monthly installments.

As a result of some of the asset and business model-related risks, the interest rate at which electric vehicles are being financed is quite high (20% or more) compared to ICE vehicle counterparts. Electric vehicles are excluded from the various financing schemes, and there are very limited financing options available with financial institutions that specifically cater to electric vehicles. Some of these are SBI Global Factors Limited's Green Car Loan, and Union Bank's Green Miles.

To tackle these issues at various levels, the following mechanisms can be undertaken:

(a) Setting up risk-sharing platforms that act as hedging mechanisms to safeguard the lending institutions (banks, fintechs, NBFCs) from the risk of loan defaults, OEM survival risks, etc.

(b) Creating a platform that brings together financiers and technology suppliers to increase the confidence of investors in electric vehicles and their allied technologies. This will be a continuous exercise to be undertaken in addition to the existing central and state-level electric vehicle policies and regulations.

(c) Promoting joint ventures between Indian OEMs with global large players in the e-mobility space will support the development of better-quality e-mobility products and services through technology transfer (new age batteries solutions, flexible power trains, etc.) and will boost the confidence of financial institutions and NBFCs in financing e-mobility and joint ventures.

Conventional or mainstream private banks and NBFCs are reluctant to enter the electric vehicle financing segment citing apprehensions around the residual vehicle value as the reason. As a result, specialized financiers have stepped in with their electric vehicle-specific, tailored financing solutions that cater specifically to the electric vehicle market. For example, few financial institutions are catering to low-income groups that are primarily the target market for three-wheeler electric vehicles. Their lending options are designed to specifically cater to people engaged in the informal sector who are traditionally excluded from the banking and lending framework. Such financiers rely heavily on tech-driven solutions (such as biometrics, psychometrics, etc.) to ease out the loan appraisal process. A multi-stakeholder approach that brings together the technology supplier (such as electric vehicle OEM), local financier, and large international financing institutions can help create a robust tech-driven lending business model on a large scale. The success of such a model will help other financial institutions to replicate the same and ultimately increase the adoption of electric vehicles in India.

(ii) **Technical assistance.** In the absence of any historical data regarding the credibility of electric vehicles concerning their residual value, business viability, etc., financial institutions are uncertain regarding lending in the electric vehicle segment.

Since electric vehicles are traditionally different from ICE vehicles, conventional automotive loan products will not be suitable for electric vehicle lending. Since electric vehicles follow a different life cycle compared to ICE vehicles, lending at the loan tenure and interest rates that apply to ICE vehicles will make the loan product unaffordable for the electric vehicle end customer.

As a result, financial institutions must develop some understanding of electric vehicle technology through some TA projects to create electric vehicle-specific loan terms and payment options. This will also apprise the financial institutions about the dynamics and trends of the electric vehicle industry globally and nationally to facilitate better decision-making.

(iii) **Original equipment manufacturers.** Electric vehicle financing is being done at much higher interest rates compared with the interest rates at which their ICE vehicle counterparts are being financed. Due to the perceived inherent risks associated with electric vehicles, financial institutions are financing only a small share of the vehicle value, i.e., a low loan-to-value ratio compared to the market average in the case of vehicle financing. This, coupled with higher insurance rates for electric vehicles and the availability of very few electric vehicle-specific loan products, is among the barriers to electric vehicle adoption.

These barriers can be catered to with the involvement of OEMs to some extent. OEMs can be involved to provide assurances to both the financier (through any guarantees) and to the end customer (through performance-related warranty) to create a more robust financing model.

A few financial institutions specifically mentioned that the lack of a strong resale or secondary market in the case of electric vehicles is a major barrier restricting the uptake of more financing projects in the clean energy domain.

Policy push for buyback through state government will help in developing the OEM-led buyback and refurbish programs; OEM-led provisions related to battery-repurposing will lead to the formation of a strong secondary market to safeguard the interests of the lender in case of a loan default.

(iv) **Blended finance.** Loan financing is highly dependent on the actual cash flows generated through operations. While conventional OEMs and tier-1 suppliers of auto parts are well-financed and have strong balance sheets, several OEMs in the e-mobility ecosystem and auto-component suppliers that fall into the SME category have been struggling to access financing primarily due to the size of their balance sheets and uncertainty regarding future operational cash flows.

The interest rates at which financial institutions are offering loans to their end customers (business or consumer loan) in the electric vehicle segment is presently quite high—particularly for NBFCs. These presently high interest rates can be brought down if the financier can source finances at lower interest rates and thereby pass on the benefit to its end customers. Improving the affordability of loans is the key to bringing e-mobility financing at par with other more mainstream technologies in the clean energy space such as solar, and solar rooftops.

Due to the perceived high risks associated with electric mobility, obtaining finance from traditional sources on commercially viable terms is difficult. Blended finance is an effective way to support projects that provide environmental and social returns to bridge the existing funding gaps.

Tailored financial solutions specific to the different product portfolios should be promoted blended finance solutions coupled with risk guarantees for two-wheelers and three-wheelers (considering the risk perception of the end user, credit profile, etc.). Financial institutions and NBFCs working in the e-mobility space when powered with risk guarantee and blended finance can support in offering these tailored solutions. This will help improve access to affordable finance to end users and can potentially revolutionize e-mobility (two-wheelers and three-wheelers) financing.

Tailored financial solutions such as long-term leasing, blended finance, battery buyback, etc. can cater to four-wheelers, commercial fleets, buses, and cargo vehicles.

(v) **Charging infrastructure business model.** The establishment of a well-connected charging network across rural areas and highways is imperative for the success of the electric vehicle model. In an early-stage market like India's, the business model of operating charging stations is weak. The high up-front costs required to set up the business and the associated lower cash inflows make the business model unviable for potential investors. Since the uptake of electric vehicles in the country is slow, the utilization level at public charging stations is expected to be low in the first few years, i.e., around <25%–30%, making it an unviable business proposition.

To develop a complete ecosystem around e-mobility, the following key factors will play an important role:

(a) Systemic policy support to help both the end consumers and the technology providers.

(b) Investments that support domestic manufacturing of vehicles, batteries, supply equipment, etc.

(c) Better access to consumer finance in the e-mobility market (especially two-wheelers and three-wheelers, a segment that is presently being driven through NBFCs).

(d) Developing new and innovative business models that thrive on public–private alliances and partnerships. Public sector companies for oil such as Indian Oil, Bharat Petroleum, etc. can forge long-term collaborations with OEMs and electric vehicle-charging manufacturers for developing the e-mobility charging infrastructure at their existing fuel refilling facilities. This will also help in improving the financial viability of these solutions.

(e) Providing financiers with an understanding of the inherent technology behind electric vehicles to bring more investor confidence will also help financiers create electric vehicle-specific loan products.

Private sector participation needs to support demand-side energy efficiency (energy efficiency and CSI technologies in India is evolving). Some private stakeholders—including financial institutions, technology solution/ service providers, etc.—have made impressive business gains in the endeavors. To establish a self-driven and sustainable market mechanism with enhanced private sector participation, some key areas need to be addressed.

Establishing an appropriate support mechanism to make the lending for energy efficiency and CSI technology commercially competitive and secure is one of them. An appropriate regulatory framework will support the development of energy performance contracting businesses and enhance private sector participation. An inclusive path forward to promote investment in energy efficiency, CSI technologies, and e-mobility can be found through private sector financial institutions (Figure 16).

Figure 16: Promoting Investment from the Private Sector

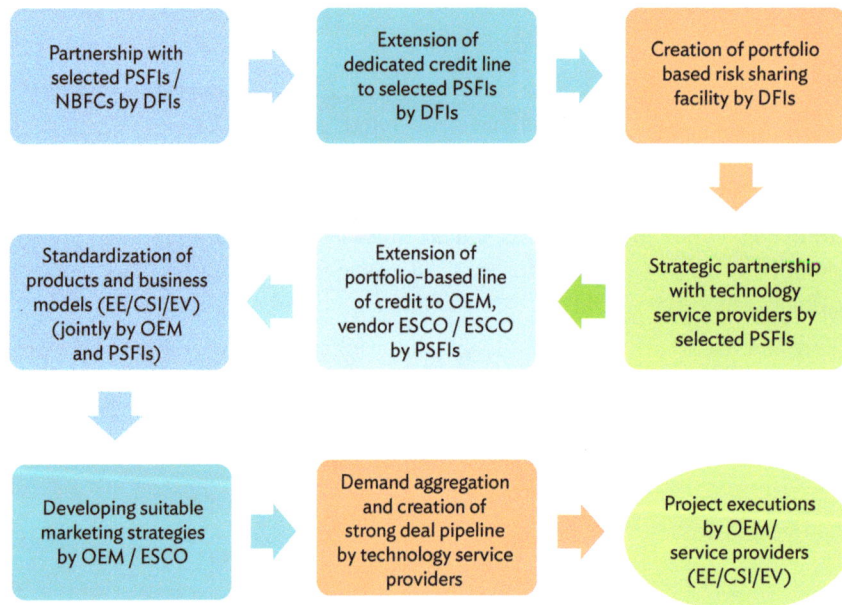

CSI = climate-smart infrastructure, DFI = development financial institution, EE = energy efficiency, ESCO = energy service company, EV = electric vehicle, NBFC = NBFC = nonbanking financial company, OEM = original equipment manufacturer, PSFI = private sector financial institution.

Source: PwC experience.

Broadly, the financing solutions can be categorized into portfolio-based risk sharing facilities, blended lines of credit, and TA. The specific challenges to be addressed differ significantly for energy efficiency, CSI, and e-mobility. Even within e-mobility, the challenges and operational context differ significantly for the two-wheeler and three-wheeler segment, and heavy vehicles (buses and trucks). The modalities and operating procedures should therefore be defined separately for each intervention to ensure effective implementation and outcomes.

Extend of a Dedicated Credit Line to Selected Private Financial Institutions by Development Financial Institutions

Commercial competitiveness of the offerings with the market is needed to gather the business demand and to grab significant business opportunities. The majority of private sector financial institutions and NBFCs are lending at a higher rate than public financial institutions.

Development financial institutions (DFIs) may extend a dedicated and long-term portfolio-based credit line at a viable rate to selected private sector financial institutions and NBFCs (who are committed to widening their deal pipeline through collaborations with OEMs and service providers of energy efficiency and e-mobility) to support building their capacities to lend at an attractive rate through blended finance.

Create a Portfolio-Based Risk-Sharing Facility by Development Financial Institutions

Keeping the offerings competitive with the market is a core need to accelerate the adoption of energy efficiency and CSI technologies. The creation of a portfolio-based risk sharing facility will help private sector financial institutions in optimizing the risk guarantee component based on needs and determined risks of the individual projects, keeping the offerings competitive.

Setting up risk-sharing platforms for e-mobility that act as hedging mechanisms will safeguard the lending institutions (banks, fintechs, NBFCs) from the risk of loan defaults and cases of business insolvency. Electric vehicles are an emerging market with higher risk, hence setting up the facility will support reducing the nonperforming assets.

DFIs may support the creation of this facility to encourage the participation of private sector stakeholders by limiting their business risks. This facility may also inclusively support both project-based and asset-based financing. The inclusion of risk guarantee coverage for asset-based financing will help to expand the range of technologies covered through this financing model that has been proven to be user-friendly and scalable.

Establish Strategic Partnerships Among Selected Private Financial Institutions and Technology Solutions and Service Providers

Building confidence in business propositions may require strategic partnerships to leverage the subject expertise of counterparts. Partnerships among stakeholders in the financial and technology supply chain will help in developing tailored products with combinational offerings for targeted consumers. This will increase the conviction around energy efficiency and CSI technologies as promising technologies for financing and will help in creating a strong deal pipeline through demand aggregation.

Private sector financial institutions, OEMs, and service providers (ESCO, e-mobility) should take the lead in building these strategic partnerships. DFIs, national public agencies, etc. may also support this endeavor by providing a common platform and bringing these stakeholders together.

Develop New and Innovative Business Models that Thrive on Public-Private Alliances and Partnerships

Private sector financial institutions and technology solutions and/or service providers (ESCO, e-mobility) should take the lead in building this alliance and developing partnerships with public departments for strengthening the ecosystem required for e-mobility. Financial institutions, electric vehicle promoters, national public agencies, state-level departments, etc. may also support this endeavor for developing financially viable solutions for electric vehicle charging (including charging, battery swapping facilities, etc.).

Standardize of Products and Business Models

Limiting the business risks through standardization of credit analysis and financing processes for specific technology solutions will help optimize the financial appraisal process and improve the overall delivery time for the end consumers. Operational efficiency is one of the keys to success. Standardization of business models for these products can drive effective results. These models will also be easier to understand for end consumers and may help in reducing the business conversion lead time.

Specialized TA projects can be provided to private sector financial institutions in standardizing the financial appraisal process and business models. OEMs and/or service providers (ESCOs) are also well-positioned to collaborate with financial institutions for this.

DFIs may support private sector financial institutions and OEMs and/or service providers in standardizing the business contracts, frameworks, tools, etc. to evaluate energy savings and resultant cash flows.

Develop Suitable Marketing Strategies for Demand Aggregation and a Strong Deal Pipeline

Once the partnerships among selected private sector financial institutions and OEMs and/or service providers (ESCOs) are established, setting out clear priorities is needed in describing their ambitions and the strategies to achieve operational excellence.

OEM and ESCO providers may play an important role in dealing with end consumers through their established marketings and sales channels and in generating demand from them. Hassle-free and easy financing will need to be ensured by the private sector financial institutions with an innovative and strategic approach.

Provide Project and/or Asset-Based Financing (Blended Financial Solutions)

Project and/or asset-based financing for energy efficiency and CSI technologies is a much more convincing business case for end consumers. Commercialized technologies with standardization are suitable to be financed with this model.

Financial institutions and NBFCs can work closely with DFIs to develop financial products with blended finance to reduce the cost of finance which can leverage the higher uptake of energy efficiency, CSI, and e-mobility projects. Loan financing is highly dependent on the actual cash flows generated through operations. The availability of lower cost of capital will support better internal rate of return and net present value.

OEMs and service providers may support private sector financial institutions in developing a list of products to be considered under this model. This will help leverage opportunities for financing these products at a much faster pace.

Promote the Participation of Women

Gender equality has always been an important aspect of DFIs. Women have a limited business share at both supply and demand ends for energy efficiency and CSI technologies. Supporting competent women entrepreneurs to ensure their greater participation in this sector will require innovative initiatives through financial institutions.

Financial institutions may consider accepting alternative collateral options including postdated checks or movable and/or business assets, etc. in case of conventional financing. Financial institutions may also consider providing customized loan offerings to women. DFIs or other leading national financial institutions may earmark dedicated funds for women to be routed through private sector financial institutions.

Summary of Proposed Actions for Key Stakeholders

To develop a focused approach for strengthening the energy efficiency and CSI ecosystem—including a strong cadre of ESCOs and a robust e-mobility ecosystem—the following actions are proposed for major stakeholders. These initiatives will help in de-linking the challenges, to support and strengthen the climate and sustainability finance framework for India. The financing framework developed will lay a strong foundation to support financing projects helping in energy and environmental conservation, which will support India to meet the short-term NDC goals set for 2030 and in achieving the long-term goal of a carbon-free economy by 2070.

Financial regulator. RBI has to play a pivotal role in inculcating the culture of prioritizing climate finance among private sector financing institutions and in devising new and innovative solutions. RBI is proactively working toward this and with a consultative approach and has floated the discussion paper to support a green taxonomy.[43] RBI may introduce energy efficiency and e-mobility as priority sector lending to sectors to support the climate agenda. The financial regulator may collaborate with NITI Aayog, the Ministry of Power, the Bureau of Energy Efficiency, and other ministries and stakeholders to seek views and suggestions while developing special climate-specific recommendations, reporting mandates, etc. to support wider adoption of energy efficiency, CSI, and e-mobility.

Relevant ministries and the Government of India. The Government of India is already supporting activities allied with sustainability and energy efficiency. The production-linked incentive scheme for batteries, renewable energy, and energy efficiency appliances are strengthening the ecosystem. Mandates on energy efficiency for industries and buildings by the Ministry of Power were instrumental to initiating the activities of energy efficiency and CSI in the country. Such mandates and periodic reviews of the regulations and modifications will support India to become a carbon-neutral economy by 2070. A series of steps are needed in the ESCO ecosystem including access to affordable finance for ESCOs, creating a robust set of rules and documentation around ESCO contracting, and the measurement and verification of savings, etc.

Development finance institutions. DFIs have been proactively supporting the climate agenda through multiple initiatives. DFIs could explore strengthening the collaboration with NBFCs and financial institutions to develop tailored and customized financial solutions for energy efficiency, CSI, and e-mobility. International development agencies can support the capacity-building activities and programs required to strengthen energy efficiency, CSI, and e-mobility financing. International development agencies can develop portfolios for climate finance through partnerships and collaborations with NBFCs and financial institutions.

---

[43]   Reserve Bank of India. n.d. Discussion Paper on Climate Risk and Sustainable Finance.

Nonbanking financial companies and financial institutions. Financial institutions are key stakeholders in the entire scheme of things. Financial institutions are beginning to recognize and respond to the importance of developing or enhancing their climate finance portfolio, given global and national priorities. They will need to actively seek collaboration with DFIs on climate finance. Areas of collaboration could include risk-sharing instruments and innovative financing instruments.

Financial institutions will also need to play a lead role in collaboratively working with ESCOs and OEMs. They can leverage the capabilities of OEMs, ESCOs, and vendor ESCOs—including their market connections—and their understanding of energy efficiency, CSI, and e-mobility technologies. The collaboration will be very useful for devising and implementing demand aggregation, customer acquisition, and pipeline creation strategies.

Another potential area for collaboration with technology and service providers is for standardization of energy efficiency, CSI, and e-mobility solutions, possibly in combination with technical assistance support through DFIs. Several NBFCs have already demonstrated the effectiveness of such collaborative approaches and are well positioned to scale up their activities.

Original equipment manufacturers, energy service companies, and vendor energy service companies. These are key stakeholders in the entire framework. OEMs, ESCOs, and vendor ESCOs typically have a sound engineering and technology base as manufacturers, project implementors, and system integrators. They are best positioned to leverage their technical know-how and market connections to create a deal pipeline in collaboration with NBFCs and financial institutions.

There are instances where ESCOs have successfully serviced lines of credit from NBFCs allowing them the comfort of generating and executing a deal pipeline asynchronously over time. This possibility should also be actively explored by ESCOs aspiring to achieve scale.

The roles of the various stakeholders are interlinked and complement each other. This study attempts to propose various solutions that are also interlinked and complementary. These are derived based on consultations with relevant stakeholders and observation of market dynamics and the successes and learnings from previous schemes and interventions. Several promising climate-smart technologies are also identified as ready reckoners for financial institutions.

It is up to the relevant private and public sector stakeholders to collaborate and arrive at a judicious mix of the proposed solutions to best leverage the significant market opportunity in the energy efficiency, CSI, and e-mobility domains. Decarbonizing the national economy is a big challenge and an even bigger opportunity. As technology and financing markets evolve in response to the important national and global priorities of climate change and decarbonization, private sector entities, including financial institutions that brace themselves for early adoption of climate-friendly and green strategies, will position themselves to make the most of the immense business opportunities.

APPENDIX 1
APPROACH AND METHODOLOGY FOR IDENTIFYING SECTORS WITH THE MOST ENERGY SAVINGS POTENTIAL

The study approach involved:

(i) Desk review of relevant knowledge documents.

(ii) Consultation with relevant stakeholders.

(iii) Detailed analysis of the stock of views and information collected through secondary research and primary consultation.

(iv) Identification of probable solutions and potential financial and/or technology partners.

An extensive review of relevant knowledge documents, including various financial schemes and policy landscape for energy efficiency and climate-smart infrastructure (CSI) technologies in targeted sectors of the economy, was carried out. Major stakeholders, including various financial institutions, technology suppliers, energy service companies, electric mobility players, etc., were consulted to draw out benefits from their views, suggestions, and feedback.

Gender sensitivity and inclusiveness was an important aspect throughout the study. The study analyzed the share and profile of women-owned or women-led businesses in targeted segments and identified the constraints they face in accessing technologies or managing the supplier dynamics that differentiate them from male-led businesses.

The methodology for identifying the sectors having the most energy savings potential used the following selection criteria:

Selection Criterion 1: Energy Consumption

Sectors were ranked based on their absolute energy consumption. A list of small and medium-sized enterprise (SME) sectors with the highest total energy consumption was prepared using data from various cluster manuals available in the public domain.

Some of the highest energy-consuming sectors in India are textiles, foundries, steel re-rolling, ceramics, and buildings. This is mainly due to the number of SME establishments in the sector using high energy compared to other sectors. Operations and processes in these sectors require higher energy consumption (energy-intensive operations such as metal melting, high-temperature heating, matching, multiple operations, etc. are carried out during the processing of the products in these sectors) for processing the unit output.

Selection Criterion 2: Energy Intensity

Clusters were ranked based on energy intensity as a percentage of production costs in typical micro, small, and medium-sized enterprise (MSME) units in clusters. Energy intensity is usually governed by sector-specific energy-consuming processes and technologies; it is also affected by the type of fuels used, the level of mechanization, etc.

Foundries and steel re-rolling mill sectors usually have the highest energy intensity, but it also depends on the type of technologies deployed in a particular subsector or SME cluster.

Selection Criterion 3: Average Energy Efficiency Potential

Sectors were ranked based on the energy savings potential from the business-as-usual scenario in a typical SME unit in the sector. This factor is mainly governed by energy reduction potential through the adoption of energy efficiency and CSI technologies, retrofits, the potential for a fuel switch, and efficient utilities applicable to the sector.

This data was prepared using data from various sector and/or cluster manuals, energy audit detailed project reports available in the public domain, and team experience in energy efficiency programmatic interventions.

Selection Criterion 4: Sector-Level Absolute Greenhouse Gas Emissions

Sectors were ranked based on the reductions in greenhouse gas (GHG) emission potential from the business-as-usual scenario by type of the MSME unit in the sector. The existing fuel mix and potential for a fuel switch, carbon dioxide conversion factors, and GHG reduction potential through the adoption of energy efficiency technologies, and retrofits were considered for estimating GHG emissions potential.

Methodology for Ranking the MSME Sectors

(i) The study estimated the value against each parameter for various sectors and provided weights to each criterion for ranking the MSME sectors.

(ii) Equal weight (0.25) was provided to each of the four parameters.

(iii) The value of 1 was assigned to the highest value in each parameter, and the value for other sectors for those parameters was proportionately calculated. **For example, if an energy intensity of 30% is highest in that category, the value "1" was assigned to that, and 15% energy intensity has been assigned (1,530x1) 0.50 value against that category**.

During consultations with technology providers and energy service companies, the study revalidated the data gathered during secondary research for mapping and short-listing the energy efficiency and CSI technologies for the SME sector (Table A1).

Table A1: Sector and Subsector Processes and Technologies

Sectors and Subsectors		Sectors and Energy Consuming Processes	
Commercial Buildings	Office complexes	**Commercial Buildings**	Space cooling
	Data centers		Water pumping
	Cold storage		Lummanaire
Forging	Open die forging	**Forging**	Metal heating
	Closed die forging		Metal forming
	Ring rolling		Heat treatment and finishing
Foundry	Precision casting	**Foundry**	Metal Preparation
	Green sand molding		Metal melting
	Shell baking		Casting
Plastics	Blow molding	**Plastics**	De moisturization (granules)
	Injection molding		Melting and forming
	Sheet/ film making		Heating and holding
Chemical and Pharma	Chemical formulation	**Chemical and Pharma**	Raw material preparation-dry mixing
	Activated pharmaceutical ingredients		Drying and Granulation
	Bulk drugs		Screening, Compression
Transport	Electric vehicle charging	**Transport**	DC fast chargers
	Battery swapping and hybrid vehicles		Fuel cells and battery storage
Paper	Recycle paper	**Paper**	Shredding and digester
	Kraft paper		Bleaching and pulping
	Writing paper		Vacuum and steam drying

Source: PWC research.

APPENDIX 2
METHODOLOGY FOR SHORT-LISTING PROMINENT TECHNOLOGIES

Selection Criterion 1: Energy Savings Potential

Technologies were ranked based on their energy savings potential. Energy savings potential for the different technologies was assessed through the review of the detailed project reports (DPRs), technology compendiums, etc. Details for each technology were revalidated through consultations with technology providers and energy service companies working in these sectors and providing similar energy efficiency and climate-smart infrastructure (CSI) solutions.

Some technologies—such as the replacement of inefficient conventional box type metal heating furnaces (fossil fuel fired) with modern, state-of-the-art insulated gate bipolar transistor induction billet heater with Internet of Things (IoT)-based control—possess higher energy savings potential compared with other technologies. Energy savings will vary from unit to unit based on the difference in operating efficiency for similar equipment or machine.

Based on secondary research and prior experience working in the small and medium-sized enterprise (SME) sectors, the study assigned a typical range of energy savings potentials for each of the technologies. The range is assigned based on the overall sector dynamics (considering variation in operating practices across SME units).

To rank the technologies based on this criterion, the average value of the range was considered.

Selection Criterion 2: Investment Potential (Ticket Size)

Technologies were ranked based on the investment potential required for implementation in the SME sector. Through the review of DPRs, technology compendiums, and consultations with technology providers, the study identified the investment range for the technologies across the SME segment. Typically, the process upgradation and/or technology switch projects are highly capital-intensive compared to simple retrofit of energy efficiency and CSI technologies and crosscutting technologies.

For example, automated high-pressure casting with robotic fettling for the foundry sector (state-of-the-art facility development) is a highly capital-intensive technology that helps in energy conservation and improvement in productivity. Switching from cupola melting furnaces to induction melting furnaces (process upgradation) is comparatively less capital intensive. Energy efficiency crosscutting technologies and utilities are generally less capital intensive compared to process technologies.

Using secondary research and experience working in the SME sector, the study categorized the investment potential into buckets or ranges applicable to the SME units. The average value of this range was considered to rank the technologies based on this parameter.

Selection Criterion 3: Replication Potential

To evaluate the comparative market size for the different energy efficiency and CSI technologies, replication potential is the key parameter to be reviewed along with investment size. During desk research, attempts were made to qualitatively capture the replication potential in the sector based on the categorizations **high, medium**, and **low**.

For example, crosscutting technologies such as an energy-efficient pump and/or screw air compressors have higher replication potential across the different sectors. These technologies, which have wider replication potential, were marked as **high** during evaluation. Subsector-specific technologies, such as new co-generation plants, have limited replication potential within the sector. These technologies are limited to specific sectors only, hence marked as **low** during evaluation. Replication potential for electric vehicle charging is high due to push from e-mobility campaigns and policy incentives.

Selection Criterion 4: Sector-Level Absolute Greenhouse Gas Emissions Reduction

Technologies were ranked based on the reductions in greenhouse gas (GHG) emission potential compared to a baseline scenario. Reduction in GHG emissions is important for moving toward a sustainable economy. During desk research, the study evaluated this criterion on a qualitative basis. Technologies that use cleaner fuels such as electricity, gas, solar, and renewable energy have higher GHG mitigation potential; these are marked as high. Energy efficiency technologies that have lower energy savings potential and use the same fuel type were marked as low during evaluation.

For example, the switch to an electric vehicle from a fossil fuel-operated vehicle or the use of an induction heating furnace in place of fossil fuel-fired metal heating furnaces possess high GHG emission reduction potential. These technologies were marked as **high** under the criterion of GHG emission reduction potential.

Selection Criterion 5: Payback

Technologies were ranked based on typical payback based on the implementation of technology in the SME sector. Through the review of DPRs, technology compendiums, and consultations with technology providers, and experience of past projects, the study defined the payback range for the technologies across the SME segment.

Typically, process upgradation and/or technology switches are highly capital intensive and have a longer payback period compared with retrofitting energy efficiency and CSI technologies and crosscutting technologies which typically have lower payback.

For example, automated high-pressure casting (state-of-the-art facility development) is a highly capital-intensive technology that helps in energy conservation and improvement in productivity having higher payback. Use of central air-conditioning and/or higher energy efficiency-labeled air conditioners also have higher payback.

Energy efficiency crosscutting technologies and/or utilities are generally less capital intensive and have lower payback periods. To rank the technologies based on this parameter, the average value of the range was considered.

Selection Criterion 6: Market Acceptance

This qualitative criterion defines the market acceptance of a particular technology as having been categorized as commercial (most accepted), semi-commercial (moderate acceptance), and state-of-the-art (lower acceptance).

Technologies that are available off-the-shelf (i) require no energy study at the unit level before implementing such technologies, (ii) have enough case studies present in the public domain that define the proven energy savings potential, and (iii) are categorized under commercial technologies. These technologies have the highest market acceptance among SMEs. For example, energy efficiency technologies such as energy-efficient pump sets, screw compressors, CSI including LED lighting, energy-efficient air-conditioning, occupancy sensors in buildings, etc.

Technologies that require customizations at the unit level are based on the energy study and baseline assessment before implementation. A lower number of proven case studies are available and categorized under the semi-commercial category. Some examples are microturbines for steam pressure to reduce power generation, and electric vehicle fleet charging infrastructure.

Technologies that do not have enough implementations in micro, small, and medium-sized enterprises (MSMEs)—specifically in the micro- and small-sized enterprises—where implementation of technologies requires significant investment but also results in huge energy savings. These technologies are categorized as **state-of-the-art**. Some examples are automated casting lines for foundries, and use of fuel cells as an energy source in the transport sector.

For example, a switch to an electric vehicle from a fossil fuel-operated vehicle, the use of induction heating furnaces in place of fossil fuel-fired metal heating furnaces possess high GHG emission reduction potential. These technologies were marked as **high** under the criterion of GHG emission reduction potential.

Replacement of inefficient pumps with an energy-efficient pump will have a limited impact on GHG emission reduction and was marked as **low** during the evaluation.

Methodology for Ranking Technologies

Rankings have been calculated separately for the following two broad categories of technologies:

(i) technologies related to energy CSI (building and transport sectors), and
(ii) technologies for the industrial sector (energy efficiency).

Calculating the Relative Rank of Each Technology Against Each Criterion

The ranking of each of the technologies was done based on the above six criteria. Weights were assigned to each criterion. During the analysis, higher weights have been assigned to the factors that are linked to the total market potential of the particular technology.

Criteria such as ticket size and replication potential broadly define the total energy efficiency potential for a particular technology. During the evaluation, a weight of 0.3 was allocated to these two factors to gauge the technologies that have higher energy efficiency potential. The four other parameters were GHG emission, payback, market acceptance, and energy savings, and are considered equally important for the adoption of energy efficiency technologies. Equal weights of 0.1 were assigned to these four factors.

Weights were assigned to different technologies for the quantitative criteria (energy savings, ticket size, and payback).

For example, energy savings of 30% is the highest in that category, with a value of "0.1" (i.e., the value of the weight for that parameter). Accordingly, 15% energy savings will be assigned (1,530x.1) 0.05 value against that category.

Weights were assigned to different technologies for the qualitative criteria (replication potential, market acceptance, and GHG emission reduction potential). Qualitative parameters were marked as **low, medium, and high** (i.e., replication potential, and GHG emission reduction potential). **High** was given the assigned weight, medium was assigned two-thirds of the assigned weight, and *low* was assigned one-third of the assigned weight.

For example, for the market acceptance criterion, commercialized technology was assigned the highest weight (0.1) and semi-commercialized was assigned a weight of 0.1/3*2 = 0.667, and state-of-the-art was assigned a value of 0.1/3 = 0.33.

Calculating the Overall Rank of Each Technology

For each technology: Cumulative weight = Summation of relative weights for all six criteria

The ranking is done corresponding to the cumulative weights, i.e., the technology with the highest cumulative weight is assigned the highest rank.

IDENTIFYING WOMEN-LED BUSINESSES IN THE CLEAN ENERGY SUPPLY CHAIN

While the various barriers, challenges, and possible solutions to encourage more women to access financing in the clean energy micro, small, and medium-sized enterprise (MSME) sector have been identified, there are case studies on different success stories of women-led businesses. These real-time business case studies will help understand how women can be involved at each step of the clean energy value chain.

With a focus on micro and small enterprises, the engagement of women within the clean energy market can be categorized as follows:

(i) **Women-owned enterprises that provide clean energy-related products and solutions**

In January 2019, a joint initiative of Shell Foundation, Zone Startups, DFID India (Government of the United Kingdom), and the Government of India, Department of Science and Technology—known as "POWERED Accelerator"—announced its support to nine women-led enterprises working in the clean energy space (Table A9.1):

Table A3: Women-Led Enterprises Working in the Clean Energy Space

S. No.	Name of Enterprise	Founder	Business Description
1	REVY Environmental Solutions	Dr. Vanita Prasad	REVY Environmental Solutions was incorporated in 2018 and is based in Gujarat, India. The company provides waste management solutions in a cost-effective and energy-efficient manner.
2	Cydee Technologies Pvt. Ltd.	Monika Jha	Cydee Technologies is based in Bengaluru, Karnataka, and was founded in 2017. It focuses on the manufacturing of energy-saving, and anti-theft solar streetlight systems.
3	DD Biosolution Technology Pvt. Ltd.	Debashree Padhi	DD Biosolution Technology was founded in Bhubaneswar, Odisha, in 2016 with a focus on producing green energy from agricultural waste to provide end-to-end cooking solutions for women in rural and semi-urban parts of the country.
4	FinEffi Energy Solutions	Bhavana Chittawar	FinEffi brings together the concepts of finance and efficiency to reduce electricity costs for homes, hotels, hospitals, and other domestic as well as commercial buildings through Internet of Things and data analytics.
5	GTarang Energy Solutions	Manvi Dhawan	GTarang was founded in Mumbai, Maharashtra, in 2018 to convert individual as well as industrial waste into useful energy.

continued on next page

Table A3 *continued*

S. No.	Name of Enterprise	Founder	Business Description
6	Pushan Renewable Energy Pvt. Ltd	Susmita Bhattacharjee	With a focus on solar energy, Pushan Renewable was founded in Indore, Madhya Pradesh, as a social enterprise that aimed to provide innovative solar-powered systems and products to generate income for women in rural parts of the country.
7	Paterson Energy Pvt. Ltd.	Vidya Amarnath	Paterson Energy was incorporated in Chennai in 2016 and works toward recycling plastic waste through the process of Plastic Thermochemical Depolymerization.
8	Prakriti Biosystems Engineering	Disha Ahuja	Prakriti Biosystems provides decentralized food waste, kitchen waste, and solid waste bio-methanation solutions. It was founded in 2019 and is based in Hyderabad, Andhra Pradesh.
9	Durga Energy	Rukmani Katara	Durga Energy is based in Rajasthan and is focused on manufacturing solar panels and other solar products. Durga actively engages women employees in the manufacturing, installation, and maintenance of solar products and solutions—thereby providing them with employment opportunities.

Source: PwC project experience.

(ii) **Women working as employees or value chain partners in clean energy enterprises**

Traditionally, women have been underrepresented as employees within the clean energy landscape, particularly in technology and engineering related roles. The inclusion of women in tech-oriented roles within the clean energy sector will not only help generate more employment opportunities but also would help create a better understanding of the customer needs to design and create more gender-inclusive products and services.

There are a few companies such as Dharma Life, Frontier Markets, etc. working in the energy efficiency space that have included women—especially rural women—as product distributors and sales agents in villages and other rural parts of the country. Dharma Life's sustainable products such as solar lights, clean cookstoves, etc. have reached 10 million beneficiaries across more than 50,000 villages in 13 states of India through its network of more than 16,000 rural women entrepreneurs.

To enable participation of women entrepreneurs in the last-mile delivery segment, businesses must provide them with the requisite training, support from other family members, safe working timings and conditions, etc. for easy commute and generate a strong customer base to be able to generate a viable income.

(iii) **Women as end users of clean energy products and services**

This category is primarily about women that are the end users of machines that are powered through clean energy-related technologies. As per a study conducted by the Council on Energy, Environment and Water, the following clean energy-based technologies are the most popular among women entrepreneurs:

(a) Solar energy-related technologies such as solar panels, solar pumps, solar lighting, etc.;

(b) E-rickshaws; and

(c) Improved cookstoves, biomass gasifiers, etc.

In July 2022, ETO Motors—one of India's leading electric mobility-as-a-service providers—announced its collaboration with the Delhi Metro together with the support of the GMR Varalakshmi Foundation and MOWO, a nongovernment organization promoting safe mobility for women. As part of the agreement, around 300 women drivers will be deployed across various metro stations located in the Delhi–NCR region to provide last-mile connectivity to commuters through ETO's sustainable and environment-friendly e-rickshaws. Electric vehicle charging stations of ETO are strategically located at various metro stations, residential societies, and other public places to enable its women drivers easy access to vehicle chargers. Further, MOWO will be responsible for the onboarding and training of women, and the entire initiative will be focused on providing continued guidance and support to women to help them become micro-entrepreneurs and thereby increase their employability.

While it is contrary to the popular perception, women-led businesses generate higher profit margins compared with that generated by businesses owned by male entrepreneurs.

Further, as per a study conducted by Bain (2019),[1] it is estimated that women-owned enterprises have the potential to generate from 150 million to 170 million new jobs by 2030. It is imperative to create a business environment that not only supports and nurtures the growth of women-led enterprises but also creates equal opportunities for women across all steps of the value chain.

Source: Bain and Company. 2019. *Powering the Economy with Her*. New Delhi.

LONG LIST OF TECHNOLOGY AND SERVICE PROVIDERS IN ENERGY EFFICIENCY, CLIMATE-SMART INFRASTRUCTURE, AND THE ELECTRIC VEHICLE ECOSYSTEM

Table A4: Mapping of the Energy Efficiency and Climate-Smart Infrastructure Technology and Service Providers

Name	Category	Unique Selling Proposition
75f	OEM	Energy management systems and buildings
ABB	OEM	Utilities - multiple sector applications / automation - CSI
Airprax Pneumatic	LSP	Compressed air solutions
Ankur Scientific	OEM	Utilities - multiple sector applications (paper, chemical, steel)
Basotra Engineers	LSP	Compressed air solutions
Battery smart	OEM	Electric vehicle battery swapping stations
Battery smart	OEM	Electric vehicle battery swapping stations
Bosch	Vendor ESCO	ESCO - energy efficiency
Bounce	OEM	Commercial fleet-electric vehicle financing and charging solutions
Desire Energy	ESCO	ESCO - energy efficiency
Electronics and Engineering Company Pvt Ltd	OEM	Textile / Automation - energy efficiency, CSI
Electrotherm / Megatherm	OEM	Steel and allied sectors
EnEFF furnaces	LSP	Heating furnaces and insulations
Eto motors	OEM	Electric vehicle fleet aggregator/service solutions
Etrio	OEM	Electric vehicle manufacturer (3W)
Exicom	OEM	Electric vehicle batteries
Gardner Denver	OEM	Utilities - multiple sector applications
ISCT	LSP	Thermal insulation solutions
Jyoti CNC	OEM	Crosscutting - multiple sectors
Kaeser	OEM	Air compressors and related energy efficiency technologies
Magenta Group	OEM	Electric vehicle charging infrastructure manufacturer
Milacron	OEM	Plastics sector - injection molding and other machinery
MoEVing	OEM	Commercial fleet, electric vehicle financing and charging solutions
NCON Turbines	OEM	Multiple sectors - thermal solutions (chemical, textile, pharma, rubber, paper etc.)

continued on next page

Table A4 *continued*

Name	Category	Unique Selling Proposition
Parker Legris	OEM	Compressed air solutions
Plasma Induction	OEM	Steel and allied sectors
Pranat Energy	Vendor ESCO	ESCO - energy efficiency, CSI
Promethean energy	Vendor ESCO	ESCO - energy efficiency
Rrdye	OEM	Electric vehicle fleet aggregator/service solutions
Saven	ESCO	ESCO - energy efficiency
Schneider Electric	OEM	Multiple sectors - energy efficiency, CSI technologies
Servotech Power Systems Pvt Ltd.	Vendor ESCO	ESCO - energy efficiency, CSI
Smart Joules	ESCO	ESCO - energy efficiency, CSI
SPG Prints	OEM	Textile / automation - energy efficiency, CSI
Thermax	OEM	Multiple sectors - energy efficiency technologies
Voltas limited	OEM	Crosscutting energy efficiency technologies and energy efficiency solutions for textiles
Yantra Harvest	ESCO	ESCO - energy efficiency, renewable energy

CSI = climate-smart infrastructure, ESCO = energy service company, LSP = local service provider, OEM = original equipment manufacturer.
Source: PwC research.

APPENDIX 5
DETAILS OF DIFFERENT SCHEMES FOR ENERGY EFFICIENCY AND CLIMATE-SMART INFRASTRUCTURE

SPEED and SPEED PLUS

(Sources: Details of the schemes are taken from the SIDBI website.)

Scheme Duration: June 2019–Ongoing

The Small Industries Development Bank of India (SIDBI) launched the SPEED and SPEED Plus schemes for machinery purchase from original equipment manufacturers (OEMs) at a competitive rate of interest. The SPEED and SPEED PLUS schemes facilitate the flow of credit to micro, small, and medium-sized enterprises (MSMEs) for investing in machinery. This scheme was launched as SPEED in June 2019. An upgraded version SPEED PLUS was also launched by SIDBI thereafter.

The scheme does not specifically focus on energy efficiency equipment. The unique selling proposition of this scheme is the quick processing time of loans. The loan processing time is less than 72 hours, which is deemed extremely suitable for MSMEs. A few observations on the scheme are as follows:

(i)   Eight OEMs signed memorandums of understanding with SIDBI; machinery purchased from these OEMs is eligible for financing; all OEMs empaneled provide the energy-efficient equipment.

(ii)   Up to 100% financing of high-end machinery; no immovable property needed as collateral; lower interest rates.

(iii)   Interest rates range from 8.80% to 10.5% with a loan tenure of up to 5 years including a moratorium of 3–6 months.

(iv)   SIDBI Term Loan Assistance for Rooftop Solar Photovoltaic Plant (STAR).

Scheme Duration: June 2019–Ongoing

SIDBI's STAR Scheme (SIDBI term loan assistance for rooftop solar photovoltaic plant) provides loans to MSME units to replace existing grid power with solar power. Eligible units can borrow up to $31,250 under this scheme to install rooftop solar plants with 25–500 kilowatts (kW) capacity.

(i)   Financing up to 100% with collateral accounting for 15%–25% of the cost of the solar photovoltaic has to be provided by the borrower in the form of the FD.

(ii)   The maximum capacity of the panel installed shall not exceed the connected load.

(iii)   Interest rates range from 9.1% to 10.2% with a loan tenure of up to 5 years including a moratorium of 3–6 months.

(iv)   The STAR scheme offers collateral-free loans for on-site rooftop solar photovoltaic plants. The scheme covers the equipment and the installation cost of the project. The unique selling proposition of the scheme as promoted by SIDBI is quick sanction and fast disbursement for eligible MSMEs. The loan is also covered by a credit guarantee.

SIDBI signed a memorandum of understanding with Tata Power for the uptake of this initiative. Tata Power is providing the financing of renewable energy installation for MSME customers of Tata Power for both off-grid and on-grid installations.

Risk Guarantee Schemes

Partial Risk Sharing Facility

(Source: SIDBI PRSF scheme)

Scheme Duration: 2015–Ongoing

The partial risk sharing facility (PRSF) was created to mobilize commercial financing for energy efficiency projects. PRSF is a Global Environment Facility (GEF)-funded project, and the implementing partners are the World Bank, SIDBI, and Energy Efficiency Services Limited (EESL). The fund is managed by SIDBI, and technical assistance is provided by EESL and/or SIDBI. All scheduled commercial banks and nonbanking financial companies (NBFCs) registered with the Reserve Bank of India (RBI) are eligible as participating financial institutions after empanelment. As of 2023, 14 financial institutions have been empaneled (Appendix 9). PRSF guarantees a maximum of 75% of the loan amount for a loan from $125,000 to $1.875 million.

The PRSF guarantee fund corpus is $37 million (₹2.74 billion); up until 2023, loans of over $18.75 million have been sanctioned for more than 35 projects under the scheme. Under PRSF, there is a provision to cover loans on the balance sheet of either the energy service company (ESCO) or the host.

A few observations on PRSF are as follows:

(i)   The scheme saw a lower uptake than expected due to the underdeveloped ESCO ecosystem as well as transaction cost and lead time increments on account of the requirement for a baseline energy study.

(ii)   No direct financial benefits for MSMEs such as interest subsidies which limits the uptake in MSMEs.

(iii)   PRSF ensured flexibility in the scheme during the implementation phase, e.g., coverage for loans disbursed on balance sheet of the host entities and not just on the ESCOs balance sheet.

(iv)   PRSF has a $6 million technical assistance component for capacity building, pipeline creation, etc.

Credit Guarantee Fund Trust for Micro and Small Enterprises

(Source: CGTSME scheme document)

Scheme Duration: May 2000–Ongoing

The Credit Guarantee Fund Trust for Micro and Small Enterprises (CGTMSE) was launched to promote the MSME sector by providing financial assistance for availing a loan of up to $250,000 without any collateral or third-party guarantee. SIDBI is the nodal agency for the implementation of the scheme. CGTMSE is not restricted to energy efficiency improvements but covers loans for diversification, expansion, and modification. There are

126 member lending institutions empaneled under the scheme which include scheduled commercial banks, specified Regional Rural Banks, SIDBI, National Small Industries Corporation Limited, North Eastern Development Finance Corporation, small finance banks, and NBFCs. Several member lending institutions are listed in Appendix 9.

The scheme covers 75% (small and medium-sized units) and 85% (micro units) of the loan amount based on the different criteria for a loan of up to $250,000, and maximum credit risk borne by CGTMSE is restricted to $187,500, i.e., 75% of the amount in default. Women-led firms are eligible for 80% of the credit risk for loan amounts of up to $250,000.

It charges annual guarantee fees varying from 1% to 3%. The scheme has been active since 2000, and is ongoing. It has emerged as a successful tool in facilitating access to formal credit sources for MSMEs. Key observations related to CGTMSE are as follows:

(i)   The scheme moved from a flat guaranteed fee structure to risk-based pricing to ensure proper due diligence of loans by the member lending institutions.

(ii)   The additional guaranteed fees associated with CGTMSE (risk guarantee scheme) are a bottleneck for higher uptake as it leaves it to the discretion of the financial institutions to decide about passing on the incidence of annual guarantee fees to the borrower.

United States Agency for International Development–Development Finance Corporation Loan Guarantee Program for Rooftop Solar in SMEs

(Source: USAID–DFC Scheme)

Scheme Duration: May 2021–Ongoing

On 18 March 2021, the United States Agency for International Development (USAID) and the US International Development Finance Corporation (DFC) announced the sponsorship of a $41 million loan portfolio guarantee to help finance investments by Indian small and medium-sized enterprises (SMEs) in renewable energy solutions.

Since SMEs pay high charges for their electricity, the focus of the guarantee program is to enable SMEs in accessing reliable power and reduce electricity expenses, by making rooftop solar a sustainable, cost-saving investment and removing the barriers associated with securing the financing needed to install rooftop panels.

USAID and DFC partnered with New York-based Encourage Capital, an environmentally focused investment firm, and two Indian NBFCs, cKers Financial and woman-owned Electronica Finance Limited (EFL), to address this challenge. Encourage Capital has invested $15 million in EFL—which will use the USAID–DFC loan portfolio guarantee to stimulate the rooftop solar market, representing a $9 billion market opportunity—for SMEs.

The credit risk guarantee is extended to the two NBFCs based on an assessment of the operations and strengths of these NBFCs and offers some flexibilities that may include, for instance, an ability to vary the extent of guaranteed cover based on the needs of each loan within the loan portfolios of these NBFCs.

FAME Scheme for E-mobility

(Sources: Government of India, Ministry of Heavy Industries, National Automotive Board; and List of Vehicles Empaneled under FAME).

Scheme Duration: 2015–2024

The first phase of the Faster Adoption and Manufacturing of (Hybrid and) Electric Vehicles (FAME) scheme in India was launched in April 2015 and was extended to March 2019. Under the policy, several benefits and incentives were extended to electric vehicle manufacturers and other related technology providers to encourage the manufacturing of electric vehicles in the country. The eligible category of vehicles under the scheme were two-wheelers, three-wheelers, four-wheelers, light commercial vehicles, heavy commercial vehicles, and retrofits.

The FAME-II policy was implemented for 3 years effective from April 2019 to March 2022 and has been extended until March 2024. The scheme lays special focus on indigenous manufacturing, advanced and emerging e-mobility technologies, infrastructure, and public transportation. This phase aims to generate demand by supporting 7,000 e-buses, 500,000 e-three-wheelers, 55,000 e-four-wheeler passenger cars (including strong hybrid), and 1 million e-two-wheelers.

The Government of India's FAME (Faster Adoption and Manufacturing of Hybrid and Electric Vehicles) scheme has been instrumental in promoting electric mobility and infrastructure development across the country. With significant budget allocations and subsidy incentives, the scheme aims to accelerate the adoption of electric vehicles and bolster the electric vehicle charging infrastructure network. Key aspects of the FAME scheme include subsidies on vehicle purchases, infrastructure development for EV charging stations in cities and on highways, and incentives for advanced batteries and registered vehicles. Below are the detailed provisions and achievements of the FAME II scheme:

(i)   The budget outlay under the FAME II scheme is $1.2 million and $66 million under FAME I.

(ii)   The government provides subsidy incentives of $200 per kilowatt-hour (with a cap of 40% of the cost of the vehicle) on the purchase of the electric vehicle. The government provides the subsidy on two-wheeler, three-wheeler, and four-wheeler vehicles.

(iii)   The government has allocated $1.2 million for electric vehicle infrastructure development. Under this part, 2,877 electric vehicle charging stations will be developed across 68 cities in 25 states and union territories, and 1,576 charging stations have been sanctioned across 9 expressways and 16 highways.

(iv)   Advanced batteries and registered vehicles will be incentivized under the scheme. A total of 166 vehicles under different categories have been registered under the FAME II scheme.

(v)   Over 303,000 vehicles have been incentivized under the FAME scheme, and incentives of over $137 million had been disbursed under FAME II up to 31 March 2022.

Past Programs on Energy Efficiency

Partial Risk Guarantee Fund for Energy Efficiency

(Source: BEE PRGFEE operational document)

Scheme Duration: May 2016–Now Withdrawn

The Partial Risk Guarantee Fund for Energy Efficiency (PRGFEE) was launched by the Government of India to promote the financing of energy efficiency projects through ESCOs in different sectors including MSMEs. The Bureau of Energy Efficiency (BEE) is the nodal agency for PRGFEE. Five financial institutions have been empaneled under PRGFEE as participating financial institutions (Appendix 9). PRGFEE guarantees up to 50% of the loan amount or $1.25 million per project, whichever is lower than the empaneled production-linked incentives for energy efficiency projects through ESCOs.

The PRGFEE fund corpus was $39 million. PRGFEE saw no uptake as of June 2023, and no loan guarantees were issued. The scheme is no longer active. A few reasons for no uptake of PRGFEE are as follows:

(i)   The ESCO ecosystem in India is underdeveloped. The lack of regulations for energy saving performance contracts and measurement and verification (M&V) protocols to simplify the energy performance contracting limits the take-up of these schemes.

(ii)   PRGF requires a baseline energy study at the MSME level, which increases the lead time and transaction cost due to energy auditing costs, resulting in a lower uptake by MSMEs.

(iii)   PRGFEE only allows loans to be taken on the balance sheet of ESCO; however, ESCOs often prefer to invest through the balance sheets of MSMEs due to their low financial credibility to repay.

(iv)   The risk coverage of 50% is on the lower side, disincentivizing the PLIs.

(v)   The scheme procedures are rigid, stringent, and extensive.

(vi)   Reimbursement to PLIs starts only after the start of legal proceedings.

Japan International Cooperation Agency–SIDBI Financing Scheme for Energy Saving Projects in MSME Sector

(Source: JICA–SIDBI Scheme for MSME)

Scheme Duration: 2008–2017

The Japan International Cooperation Agency (JICA)–SIDBI financing scheme utilized a list-based approach to encourage MSME units to undertake energy saving investments in plant and machinery to reduce energy consumption, enhance energy efficiency, reduce carbon dioxide emissions, and improve the profitability of the units in the long run.

It disbursed the line of credit of $1.5 billion to more than 5,000 MSMEs through SIDBI under three phases of the project. A list of more than 900 energy efficiency equipment eligible for financing was developed under the scheme covering more than 20 sectors. The JICA–SIDBI program is a pioneer program in energy efficiency financing. The key observations of the program are as follows:

(i)   Quick sanction and disbursement with no need for baseline study and energy audit at MSME premises.

(ii)   A list of energy efficiency technologies accompanied by a description of the technology and cost-benefit analysis helped MSMEs make informed decisions on technology adoption.

(iii) A list of energy efficiency technologies and equipment, vendors, and equipment suppliers developed by the program was updated regularly.

(iv) Provision of soft loans with lower interest rates, moratorium periods, and longer loan tenure.

(v) The operationalization of the scheme initially required significant effort in terms of capacity building of the bank's operational staff across their network in India.

Financing Energy Efficiency at MSME–World Bank–Global Environment Facility (SIDBI, BEE)

(Source: SIDBI GEF programme)

Scheme Duration: May 2010–May 2019

Financing Energy Efficiency at MSMEs (FEEM) was a Global Environment Facility (GEF)-funded project, with a budget of $63.61 million. It aimed to increase the demand for energy efficiency investments in target MSME clusters and to build their capacity to access commercial finance. The GEF implementing agency was the World Bank, and it was jointly executed by BEE and SIDBI.

The project was focused on four components:

(i) Activities to build capacity and awareness

(ii) Activities to increase investment in energy efficiency

(iii) Knowledge management

(iv) Project management support

FEEM was conceived to complement the World Bank's engagement with the Government of India on the $520 million International Bank for Reconstruction and Development (IBRD)-funded SME Finance and Development Project. The GEF-funded FEEM was designed to increase the flow of capital for energy efficiency measures and address institutional weaknesses and capacity constraints of financial institutions that restricted them from supporting MSMEs. The primary aim of the GEF-funded FEEM program was to:

(i) Increase demand for energy efficiency investments in target MSME clusters.

(ii) Build the capacity of MSMEs to access commercial finance.

The FEEM project has made significant strides in enhancing energy efficiency across various sectors in India. By training a substantial number of experts and professionals, preparing numerous detailed project reports, and facilitating substantial investments in energy efficiency initiatives, FEEM has played a pivotal role in promoting sustainable practices. Notably, the project's support for SIDBI's 4E scheme and the provision of performance-linked grants underscore its commitment to fostering innovation and efficiency in energy management. Below are some key achievements of the FEEM project:

(i) A total of 1,120 experts from 75 financial institutions and 750 energy audit professionals were trained to develop energy audit reports based on which commercial finance could be sought.

(ii) Around 1,257 investment grade detailed project reports were prepared exceeding the initial target of 730.

(iii) A total of $41 million direct energy efficiency investments emerged from the project.

(iv) Performance-linked grants were given to 67 early adopters.

(v) The project supported SIDBI's end to end energy efficiency (4E) scheme. The World Bank-supported revolving fund provided a maximum interest subsidy of 2.50% (increased to 3.58%).

Technical Assistance Schemes

Promoting Market Transformation for Energy Efficiency in Micro, Small, and Medium-Sized Enterprises: UNIDO–GEF (Energy Efficiency Services Limited, Ministry of Micro, Small and Medium Enterprises)

(Source: EESL Scheme document)

Scheme Duration: February 2010–Ongoing

Promoting market transformation for energy efficiency in MSMEs is a GEF-funded project aimed to promote the implementation of energy efficiency in the MSME sector, create and sustain a revolving fund mechanism to ensure replication of energy efficiency measures in the sector, and address the identified barriers for scaling-up energy efficiency measures and consequently promote a cleaner and more competitive MSME industry in India. The project is jointly conceptualized by the Ministry of Micro, Small and Medium Enterprises (MoMSME), GEF implementing agency (United Nations Industrial Development Organization [UNIDO]), and is being executed by EESL. The project budget is $31.3 million.

The project focuses on three components:

(i)   Program to identify energy-intensive clusters and replicable technologies,

(ii)   Demonstration projects and aggregation of demand for demonstrated technologies in the clusters, and

(iii) Financial models to support replication of energy efficiency projects in MSME.

The project focuses on both the demand-side and supply-side barriers. The project aims to create demand by undertaking demonstration projects and developing detailed project reports in identified clusters as well as developing a revolving fund that can be used to undertake energy efficiency projects in MSMEs.

The project is still in its early stage of implementation. Before the coronavirus disease (COVID-19) pandemic, the project was able to conduct scoping studies, energy audits, and identification of technologies. The conceptualization of the revolving fund has been done and the operationalization is expected soon.

Promoting Energy Efficiency and Renewable Energy in Selected Micro, Small, and Medium-Sized Enterprise Clusters in India

(Source: BEE UNIDO GEF initiative)

Scheme Duration: April 2011–Ongoing

Promoting energy efficiency and renewable energy in MSMEs in India is a GEF-funded project aimed at introducing energy efficiency technologies and enhancing the use of renewable energy technologies in process applications in energy-intensive MSMEs in five sectors (brass, ceramics, dairy, foundries, and hand tools). The GEF executing partner is UNIDO and other executing partners are the BEE, MoMSME, and the Ministry of New and Renewable Energy.

The project has four main components:

(i)   Increased capacity of energy efficiency and renewable energy product suppliers, service providers, and finance providers to support the expansion of energy efficiency and renewable energy in the clusters.

(ii)   Increasing the level of end-use demand and implementation of energy efficiency and renewable energy technologies and practices by MSMEs.

(iii) Scaling up of the project to a national level.

(iv)   Strengthening policy, institutional, and decision-making frameworks.

A few important achievements of the scheme are the following:

Table A5: Achievements of the Project

21 Pilot projects implemented, 300 DPRs developed	20,000+ tons of oil equivalent annual energy savings
600+ energy efficiency and renewable energy measures implemented	$6.62 million in monetary savings
95 Workshops organized with	$7.19 million cofinancing
300+ case studies prepared	122,838 tons of annual carbon emissions avoided

DPR = detailed project report.
Source: BEE EE financing initiatives.

Financing Energy Efficiency Programme (Bureau of Energy Efficiency)

(Source: BEE EE financing initiatives)

Scheme Duration: 2015–Ongoing

The Energy Efficiency Financing Platform (EEFP) and Framework for Energy Efficient Economic Development are two major components of the financing energy efficiency program under the National Mission for Enhanced Energy Efficiency (NMEEE) to strengthen the financing framework for energy efficiency, which is being executed by BEE.

The EEFP component aims to establish a platform to interact with financial institutions, project developers, and other stakeholders for the implementation of energy efficiency projects and accelerating energy efficiency financing. The broader objective of the scheme is to build greater knowledge and confidence through a training program within the financial sector on energy efficiency financing.

The Framework for Energy Efficient Economic Development component is envisioned with the objective of developing fiscal instruments to promote energy efficiency. It is also designed to provide comfort to lenders with the provisions of risk guarantee for performance contracts.

A few important activities initiated by BEE under EEFP are as follows:

(i)   **Grading energy efficiency projects** will increase the confidence of financial institutions toward the bankability of projects and techno-economics. Financial institutions will be able to identify, assess, and financially evaluate energy efficiency loan applications better as the overall assessment would be executed by empaneled grading agencies and the project would be given grading. BEE has planned multiple activities under this initiative to foster energy efficiency financing:

     (a)   Under this component, BEE shall reimburse the actual cost of grading (presently not exceeding $3,700 per project, for 100 projects).

     (b)   BEE has empaneled two financial institutions—Yes Bank and the Indian Renewable Energy Development Agency (IREDA)—for promoting this initiative.

     (c)   BEE is in the process of empaneling independent grading agencies (e.g., CRISIL, ICRA, etc.) as well as financial institutions for this activity.

(iv) **BEE is supporting the development of the facilitation center**, which will assist financial institutions in confirming whether loans are energy efficiency loans and will also create a pipeline of energy efficiency projects through marketing and promotion activities. The center will also facilitate identifying energy efficiency technologies for financial institutions and will develop digital platforms to connect with financial institutions and get regular energy efficiency financing-related inputs.

(v) **BEE has been working on developing a special purpose vehicle** with the support of the Power Finance Corporation/Rural Electrification Corporation to roll out different financing programs such as interest subsidy, capital subsidy, and risk guarantee. Once the special purpose vehicle is operationalized, it will support the wider spectrum of energy efficiency financing in MSMEs. The energy efficiency financing including incentive schemes, credit guarantee facilities, etc. can be availed by eligible energy efficiency projects including the project pipeline created through other initiatives under this programmatic intervention.

(vi) BEE supports multiple initiatives for promoting energy efficiency finance through various activities such as investment bazaars, and energy efficiency project pipeline creation for financial institutions.

(vii) BEE, along with nationalized banks and a few public financial institutions, has started the initiative where BEE is supporting the banks and financial institutions s with the required personnel (one financial expert and one technical expert) for energy efficiency financing activities. These initiatives will foster the strengthening of the energy efficiency portfolio of financial institutions such as SBI Global Factors Limited energy efficiency portfolio for housing, and Yes Bank sustainable finance interventions for the MSME sector.

Other Programs on Energy Efficiency and Technology Upgradation Supported by Ministries

(Source: Schemes from MoMSME)

Technology Upgradation Funding Scheme

Scheme Duration: 1999–Ongoing

The Technology Upgradation Funding Scheme (TUFS) was launched to upgrade and modernize the Indian Textile Industry by encouraging it to undertake and adopt modern technological processes or undertake capacity expansion. Since its inception, TUFS has propelled investment of more than $30 billion.

The nodal agencies under the scheme are (i) the textile industry (excluding MSMEs)–IDBI Bank, (ii) MSME textile sectors–SIDBI, and (iii) the jute industry (Industrial Finance Corporation of India [IFCI]). A listing of nodal agencies, nodal banks, and co-opted private sector commercial banks of SIDBI that were participants in the scheme is provided in Appendix 9.

Key observations of TUFS are the following:

(i) Due to the simplistic list-based approach of the scheme, the earlier schemes observed significant uptake, but the amended scheme has not seen similar results.

(ii) TUFS was revised and upgraded to incorporate large players and encourage them to bring in new investments in the sector.

(iii) During the stakeholder consultations, it was pointed out that the elaborate verification process adopted by the revised versions to curb discrepancies has led to a decrease in the uptake of the scheme.

Technology Upgradation Scheme for Micro, Small, and Medium-Sized Enterprises

Scheme Duration: 2010–2017

The Technology Upgradation Scheme for Micro, Small, and Medium-Sized Enterprises (TEQUP) scheme was launched as one of the components of the National Manufacturing Competitiveness Programme. The objective of the scheme is to sensitize and encourage the manufacturing MSME sector in India to use energy efficient technologies and manufacturing processes to reduce costs of production and GHG emissions. The second objective of the scheme is to create awareness and encourage MSMEs to acquire product certification and licenses from national and international bodies.

The Program (TEQUP) plays a crucial role in incentivizing the adoption of energy efficiency technologies and promoting quality standards in India. Through its subsidy programs, TEQUP supports businesses by covering up to 25% of project costs for implementing energy efficiency technologies. Additionally, it facilitates substantial subsidies for obtaining national and international product certifications, encouraging businesses to meet rigorous quality standards. These initiatives aim to enhance competitiveness, foster innovation, and drive sustainable practices across industries.

(i)   TEQUP provides a subsidy of up to 25% (maximum $12,500) of the project cost for the implementation of energy efficiency technology.

(ii) It also provides a subsidy of up to 75% ($1,875 for national certification and $2,500 for international certification) of the actual expenditure incurred for obtaining product certification licenses.

SIDBI is the nodal implementing agency for this scheme, and Canara Bank, Bank of Baroda, Punjab National Bank, Bank of India, and State Bank of India are the nodal banks. As of 2019–20 (no new applications after 2017), around 1,188 MSMEs had been beneficiaries of the scheme availing a subsidy of $11 million.

The TEQUP scheme has since been subsumed by the Credit Linked Capital Subsidy Technology Upgradation Scheme.[1] Overall, the TEQUP scheme has seen a low uptake. The key observations are as follows:

(i)   As per discussion with convened stakeholders and based on long-term interactions with MSME units, it has been observed that the low uptake of the scheme could be attributed to primarily the lack of promotion and awareness of the scheme among MSMEs and bankers; and

(ii) Scheme requirements such as an energy audit report (DPR) increase the transaction cost and lead time for the project.

Credit Linked Capital Subsidy Scheme

Scheme Duration: October 2000–March 2021 (under revision as of 2023)

The Credit Linked Capital Subsidy Scheme (CLCSS) facilitates subsidies to 51 subsectors and products including Khadi and Village Industries. The CLCSS provides a capital subsidy of 15% on actual term loans sanctioned and disbursed, with a maximum limit of an eligible loan of $125,000 (maximum of 1 subsidy).

---

[1]   SIDBI. 2020. *Annual Report 2019–2020*. Uttar Pradesh.

All scheduled commercial banks, scheduled cooperative banks (including the urban cooperative banks co-opted by the SIDBI), regional rural banks, state financial corporations, and Northeastern Development Financial Institution are eligible as primary lending institutions under this scheme after they execute a general agreement with any of the nodal agencies.

Key observations of the CLCSS are as follows:

(i) The CLCSS has been a long-standing and popular scheme. The scheme is not exclusive to energy efficiency and targets modernization and technology upgradation. It has been widely disseminated through a comprehensive list of primary lending institutions. The scheme is well known among the MSMEs, and many have availed benefits. The list-based approach simplifies the loan appraisal process. MSME units can only avail of a maximum ₹1,500,000 of subsidy, which is utilized by most of the MSMEs.

(ii) These observations and broad applicability are the major reasons for the excellent uptake. All allocated funds were disbursed under the scheme covering 65,000 beneficiaries with a disbursement of ₹500 million in funds.

OBSERVATIONS FROM EXISTING SCHEMES TO EXPAND LENDING FOR LOW-CARBON TECHNOLOGIES

Energy efficiency in small and medium-sized enterprises (SMEs) has been a difficult segment on account of inherent issues with energy efficiency projects and the intrinsic issues associated with the SME sector. A study performed by the Reserve Bank of India in 2019 identified the main weakness of the SME sector in the areas of access to credit, reliable capital, payment cycles, access to market, infrastructure, adoption of new technologies, and skill level of the workforce.[1]

Access to finance is one of the main barriers for the micro, small, and medium-sized enterprise (MSME) sector. The reasons for limited access to finance can be attributed to the requirement of collateral and/or guaranteeing high interest rates due to high perceived risks, rigid lending policies, complex procedures, and limited knowledge.

Energy efficiency has traditionally struggled in India due to the complexities associated with energy efficiency projects. The challenges of energy efficiency in SMEs include a limited awareness and technical knowledge of MSMEs, limited in-house technical capacities of financial institutions to evaluate energy efficiency proposals, small ticket size and high transaction cost, technology performance risk, complexities associated with energy baseline, and limited ecosystem for energy service companies (ESCOs) in India.

Moreover, energy efficiency is lower on the priority list of MSMEs compared to large industries or other businesses.

The various initiatives detailed above have attempted to proliferate energy efficiency in MSMEs through different mechanisms. It is understood that there cannot be one solution for a sector of this magnitude and spread. There have been improvements because of the efforts made by the government and various overseas development agencies; however, market transformation is yet to be seen.

---

[1]   Reserve Bank of India. 2019. Expert Committee on Micro, Small and Medium Enterprises. Press release. 18 March.

State-Led Schemes and Incentives for E-mobility

In addition to the central-level schemes and policies, several states have formulated their electric vehicle-related policies and regulations as detailed below:

Table A6.1: State-Led Initiatives for E-mobility

S. No.	State Name	Policy objectives
1	Andhra Pradesh Electric Vehicle Policy (2018)	• Aim to have 1 million electric vehicles on the road by 2024 • Allocate 200–400 hectares of land to develop electric vehicle parks • 100% reimbursement on stamp duty on the purchase of land for electric vehicle production • Make Andhra Pradesh a global hub for electric mobility development and manufacturing • Active investment through grants and venture funds to fund research, start-ups, incubators, etc. • Active investment in green technologies such as charging infrastructure, battery-swapping, hydrogen generation, etc. • Develop a skilled labor force well-versed in the electric vehicle ecosystem • Enable the transition to more environment-friendly cities
2	Bihar Draft Electric Vehicle Policy (2019)	• Aim to convert all paddle-run rickshaws to e-rickshaws by 2022 • Aim to make Bihar a preferred destination for electric vehicle-related investments • Create a manufacturing hub within the state • Aim to create fast charging stations at every 50 kilometers on state and national highways within the state
3	Delhi Electric Vehicle Policy (2020)	• For electric two-wheelers, a purchase incentive of $62.50 per kilowatt-hour (kWh) of battery capacity will be provided per vehicle to the registered owner and subject to a maximum incentive of $375 per vehicle • For electric autos, a purchase incentive of $375 per vehicle will be provided by Government of National Capital Territory of Delhi to the registered owner • For electric buses, a purchase incentive of $375 to the first 10,000 e-carriers to be registered in Delhi after the issue of the policy • For electric four-wheelers, a purchase incentive of $62.50/kWh of battery capacity will be provided (to a maximum of $1,875 per vehicle) to the registered owners of the first 1,000 e-cars to be registered in Delhi after the issue of the policy • Government of National Capital Territory of Delhi will provide a 100% grant for the purchase of charging equipment up to $75 per charging point for the first 30,000 charging points
4	Karnataka Electric Vehicle Policy (2017)	• Aim to make Karnataka a preferred destination for electric vehicle manufacturing • Aim to attract investments worth more than $3.75 billion in the electric vehicle ecosystem and to create employment opportunities for more than 55,000 people • Incentives and concessions to be provided to all charging infrastructure providers • Aim to establish a venture capital fund to encourage e-mobility-related start-ups
5	Kerala Electric Vehicle Policy (2019)	• Aim to target 1 million electric vehicles on the road by 2022 • Create a special fund to support local manufacturing of electric vehicles • Priority allotment of land and speedy execution of land allotment for local manufacturers of electric vehicles • Promote shared e-mobility and clean transportation practices within the state
6	Maharashtra Electric Vehicle Policy (2021)	• Under this policy, the state aims to incentivize the following number of vehicles under each vehicle category: • Electric two-wheeler: 100,000 • Electric three-wheeler auto: 15,000 • Electric four-wheeler cars: 10,000 • Electric four-wheeler carrier: 10,000 • Electric buses: 1,000

continued on next page

Table A6.1 *continued*

S. No.	State Name	Policy objectives
7	Tamil Nadu Electric Vehicle Policy (2019)	• Aim to attract investments worth $6.25 billion • Aim to create infrastructure for electric vehicle charging • The state offers 100% reimbursement of goods and services tax paid on the sale of electric vehicles manufactured in the state • In addition to that, there is a 15% capital subsidy on intermediate products used for manufacturing, a 100% electricity tax exemption for manufacturing industries, a 100% stamp duty exemption for transactions related to electric vehicle manufacturing, a 50% land subsidy, etc.

Sources: Andhra Pradesh State's EV policy; Bihar State's EV policy; Delhi State's EV policy; Karnataka State's EV policy; Kerala State's EV Policy; Maharashtra State's EV policy; and Tamil Nadu State's EV policy.

Schemes by Different Financial Institutions for Promoting Women Entrepreneurs

While such reforms and policy interventions are required in the long and short term, few banks and financial institutions have tailored lending products that are aligned with the needs of women-owned businesses (Table A6.2).

Table A6.2: List of Schemes by Financial Institutions for Women Entrepreneurs

S. No	Bank	Scheme	Description
1	Bank of India	Priyadarshini Yojana	This scheme was announced in 2006 by the Bank of India to provide loans to women entrepreneurs without any collateral for an amount of up to $6,250. The scheme also allowed women to avail of loans at highly subsidized rates of interest.
2	Central Bank of India	Cent Kalyani	This scheme was launched by the Central Bank of India for existing and new women entrepreneurs who are operating in the MSME space. It aims to provide financial assistance to women-owned businesses by providing loans for capital expenditure as well as for working capital. To avail of this loan, no collateral or guarantors are required.
3	Dena Bank	Dena Shakti	Under this scheme, women entrepreneurs can avail of loans of up to $25,000 at a concession of 0.25% on the interest rate. Under this, both working capital and term loans can be availed with a flexible repayment tenure that can last up to 10 years.
4	Oriental Bank of Commerce	Orient Mahila Vikas Yojana	This scheme allows women with ownership of 51% share capital either individually or jointly in a proprietary concern to avail loans. The scheme provides concession on the rate of interest of up to 2%.
5	State Bank of India	Stree Shakti Package	Under this scheme, women entrepreneurs can avail of loans of up to ₹ 2,500,000 at low rates of interest. Under the scheme, no collateral is required for a loan of up to $12,500.
6	Small Industries Development Bank of India	Mahila Udyam Nidhi	This scheme allows women entrepreneurs to avail of loans for project costs not exceeding $12,500. Under this scheme, a soft loan limit of up to 25% of the project cost, subject to a maximum of $3,175 per project, is provided to women entrepreneurs.

$ = United States dollar; ₹ = Indian rupee; MSME = micro, small, and medium-sized enterprises.
Source: PwC project experience.

APPENDIX 7
DISCUSSION GUIDE FOR TECHNOLOGY PROVIDERS

The study circulated discussion guides and questionnaires to the stakeholders well in advance to seek inputs. The questionnaire was designed to cover the following details concerning financial institutions to understand their outlook toward the clean energy financing domain particularly for small and medium-sized enterprises (SMEs) in India:

(i)   types of targeted customers (large businesses, manufacturing SMEs, commercial buildings, etc.);

(ii) breakdown of the portfolio within the SME category (i.e., the share of SMEs within the total loan portfolio);

(iii) understanding the average ticket size of loans availed;

(iv) understanding the category of loans offered (business loans, working capital loans, asset financing loans, etc.);

(v)   challenges of financing clean energy projects; and

(vi) understanding whether the financial institution has prepared any strategies specific to climate finance, whether any additional support is required to boost clean energy financing, and the financial institution's willingness to collaborate with the Asian Development Bank over the same.

Figure A7.1: Discussion Guide for Technology Providers and Energy Service Companies

Briefing to the respondent

Greetings!!

PricewaterhouseCoopers Private Limited has been commissioned by Asian Development Bank (ADB) to understand the Clean Energy Financing Opportunities for Financial Institutions for SME in India. Given your experience and expertise in this sector, we request you to be part of this discussion.

Your response will be used to develop a broad understanding of SME financing in Energy Efficiency, Renewable Energy and Electric Mobility space and will be treated in the strictest confidence and information gathered will be shared only with ADB, the beneficiary of the study. Any personally identifiable information shall not be disclosed.

S.No	Particulars	Details			
1)	Contact details/ Business Card	Name Tel & Mobile: Email: _____		Address:	
2)	Commissioning year				
3)	Name of Associated Bank(s) and FIs				
4)	Major source of finance for EE & SI availed by SMEs	Personal Finance	SIDBI/ Other Schemes	Leading Private and PSU Banks	Other NBFC
5)	Major historic type of Client finance	Loan or other		Please provide details	
6)	Number of EE & SI unit sales under financial year (2021)				
7)	Type of Sector / Sub-Sectors served	• Buildings (Commercial, Residential) • Automotive (Including EVs) • Others_____		• Industries (EE technologies) • Renewable Energy (Solar)	
8)	Key selling points of EE/ SI equipment/technology	• Fuel Cost Savings • Lower payback • EE related Vendor Accreditation • Others		• Productivity improvement • Higher IRR and NPV • GHG emission reductions	

continued on next page

Figure A7.1 *continued*

S No	Particulars	Details		
9)	Type of EE/ SI technologies	• Process Technologies • Utilities • EV supplies/ chargers • Solar PV	• Building Appliances / material • Energy Monitoring • Automation Equipment • Others	
10)	List of technologies (Product portfolio)	Provide detail product portfolio		
11)	Have you successfully implemented EE/SI projects under any schemes?	• PRSF (Partial risk sharing facility) • SPEED (SIDBI – Loan for Purchase of Equipment for Enterprise's Development) • SMILE (Soft Loan Fund for Micro Small and Medium Enterprises)	• WB-GEF (World Bank Global environment fund) • UNIDO – GEF • EESL	
12)	Preferred business model? And Why	• Capex • Opex • Others	• ESCO • Leasing	
13)	Major barriers in adopting EE / SI measures?	• Techno-commercial feasibility of EE technologies • Higher upfront cost of EE/ SI equipment • Lack of awareness among the customers • Policy / regulatory barriers in adopting solutions • Lack of incentives and subsidies for EE/ SI adoptions		
14)	Which would be motivating factor for adopting EE & SI technologies adoption by commercial and SME firms	• Energy cost savings • Ease of bank financing • Subsidies and incentives • GHG emission reductions	• Productivity improvement • Environmental related compliances • Technology demonstrations • Others	
15)	Which financing mode is preferred by commercial firms/ SMEs to implement EE/ SI measures?	Capital Investment through		
		Self-finance/ WC loan	Energy Savings Companies (ESCOs)	Term Loans through FIs

capex = capital expenditure, EE = energy efficiency, ESCO = energy service company, EV = electric vehicle, FI = financial institution, GHG = greenhouse gases, IRR = internal rate of return, JICA = Japan International Cooperation Agency, NBFC = nonbanking financial company, NPV net present value, opex = operating expenses, PV = photovoltaic, RE = renewable energy, SI = smart infrastructure, SIDBI = Small Industries Development Bank of India, SMEs = small and medium-sized enterprises.

Source: Prepared by PwC.

Figure A7.2: Technology Provider Recipients of the Discussion Guide

Name	Type	Consultation Conducted	Discussion Guide Shared
75f	OEM	✓	✓
ABB	OEM		✓
Ankur Scientific	OEM		✓
Balsotra Pneumatic	LSP	✓	✓
Battery smart	OEM		✓
Bosch	Vendor ESCO		✓
Bounce	OEM		✓
Cosmoright Consultancy Services Pvt. Ltd	ESCO	✓	✓
Design X	OEM	✓	✓
Desire Energy	ESCO	✓	✓
Electronics and Engineering Company Pvt Ltd	OEM		✓
Electrotherm/Interpower/Megatherm	OEM		✓
EnEFF	LSP		✓
Eto motors	OEM	✓	✓
Etrio	OEM		✓
Exicom	OEM		✓
Gardner Denver / Others	OEM		✓
Grundfos	OEM		✓
ISCT	LSP	✓	✓
Jyoti CNC	OEM		✓
Kaeser	OEM	✓	✓
Magenta Group	OEM	✓	✓
Milacron	OEM		✓
MoEVing	OEM	✓	✓
NCON Turbines	OEM	✓	✓
P2P	OEM	✓	✓
Parker Legris	LSP		✓
Plasma Induction	OEM	✓	✓
Pranat Energy	Vendor ESCO		✓
Promethean energy	Vendor ESCO	✓	✓
Rrdye	OEM	✓	✓
Saven	ESCO		✓
Schneider Electric	OEM	✓	✓
Servotech Power Systems Pvt Ltd.	Vendor ESCO		✓
Smart Joules	ESCO	✓	✓
SPG Prints	OEM		✓
Thermax	OEM		✓
Voltas limited	OEM		✓
Yantra Harvest	ESCO	✓	✓

ESCO = energy service company, LSP = local service provider, OEM = original equipment manufacturer.

Source: PwC project experience.

DISCUSSION GUIDE FOR FINANCIAL INSTITUTIONS

The discussion guide (questionnaire) for financial institutions is provided in Figure A8.1.

Figure A8.1: Discussion Guide for Financial Institutions

Briefing to the respondent

Greetings!!

PricewaterhouseCoopers Private Limited has been commissioned by Asian Development Bank (ADB) to understand the Energy Efficiency and Energy Smart Infrastructure Opportunities for Financial Institutions for SME in India. Given your experience and expertise in this sector, we request you to be part of this discussion.

Your response will be used to develop a broad understanding of SME financing in EE space and will be treated in the strictest confidence and information gathered will be shared only with ADB, the beneficiary of the study. Any personally identifiable information shall not be disclosed.

S.No	Particulars	Details	
Basic information and EE & SI exposure details			
1)	Bank Name:	Contact Person: Designation: Vertical: Type : Commercial Bank / NBFC / FI	Branch and address: Tel & Mobile: Email: _____
2)	Which sectors your branch cover ?	SME Sectors _____ Buildings and SI _____	
3)	Type of industrial customers?	☐ Large businesses ☐ Manufacturing SMEs Others_____	☐ Non-manufacturing SMEs ☐ Shopkeepers ☐ Commercial building
4)	Credit uptake by category of MSMEs	Please mention the share of loans availed by each category of SMEs ☐ Small _____ (in%) ☐ Medium _____(in%)	
5)	Average ticket size of EE of SI loans	☐ <5 lacs ☐ 5 to 20 lacs	☐ 20 to 50 lacs ☐ >50 lacs
6)	Challenges in financing EE / SI projects for SME?	☐ Low ticket size of EE/ SI loans ☐ Realizations of energy cost savings from EE/ SI equipment implementations ☐ Post verification of energy savings and GHG reductions from EE/ SI implementations ☐ Technicalities associated with project appraisal of EE technologies ☐ Lack of standardization in assessment of EE proposals ☐ Others_____	
Information on EE & SI financing			
7)	Type of Financing offered for EE & SI financing?	☐ Asset financing ☐ Business Loans	☐ Working capital loans ☐ Personal loans

continued on next page

Figure A8.1 *continued*

S.No	Particulars	Details	
8)	Type of loans under asset financing category?	☐ Equipment/ Machinery ☐ Plant expansion ☐ E-mobility	☐ Import of new technologies ☐ Solar PV / Solar heating ☐ EE building and Space cooling
9)	Loan exposure to Commercial firms and SMEs	☐ <10% ☐ 10 to 30%	☐ 30% to 60% ☐ >60%
10)	Number to loans SMEs (EE & SI loans; Calendar year 2021)		
11)	Prior Experience of working with suppliers of EE/ SI technologies?	☐ Loans to OEMs/ Suppliers for EE/ SI implementations at SMEs ☐ Technology vendors empaneled under past interventions- JICA SIDBI, SPEED ☐ ESCO based financing for Energy performance contracting projects- PRSF etc. ☐ Others	
12)	Percentage of loan portfolio associated with EE or SI technologies	☐ <5% ☐ 5 to 10%	☐ 10% to 20% ☐ >20%
Additional support and collaboration for fostering EE &SI finance to SMEs			
13)	Strategy / Plan related to Climate Finance ? Which EE/ SI related schemes your bank is associated with?	☐ Any ongoing initiative in EE, RE Climate ☐ Initiatives planned for EE, RE, Climate ☐ Credit lines/ Revolving funds	☐ Risk sharing mechanism- i.e. PRSF(Partial risk sharing facility) ☐ Specific solutions for women-led SME
14)	Additional support required to boost EE & SI financing?	☐ Handholding required to scale up EE financing (product design, credit methods, other – please elaborate) ☐ Empaneling with technology vendors and identification of suitable technology partners ☐ Support for developing EE instruments- ESCO, Credit line etc for SMEs ☐ Other support for Technical Assistance (TA) activities for EE & SI projects ☐ elaborate _____	
15)	Willingness for associating with ADB?	Interest in empanelling and signing TA with ADB to gain support for building on /expanding FI strategy to grow the EE and SI portfolio. Indicative interest in also working with ADB for financial product support to scale the EE and SI portfolio – if so, which instrument (funding, guarantees to de-risk portfolio)	

capex = capital expenditure, EE = energy efficiency, ESCO = energy service company, EV = electric vehicle, FI = financial institution,
GHG = greenhouse gases, IRR = internal rate of return, JICA = Japan International Cooperation Agency,
NBFC = nonbanking financial company, NPV net present value, opex = operating expenses, PV = photovoltaic, RE = renewable energy,
SI = smart infrastructure, SIDBI = Small Industries Development Bank of India, SMEs = small and medium-sized enterprises.
Source: Prepared by PwC.

Figure A8.2: Financial Institution Recipients of the Discussion Guide

Name	Type	Consultation conducted	Discussion guide shared
Akasa Financial Services	NBFC	✓	✓
Axis Bank	FI		✓
Caspian Impact Investments	NBFC	✓	✓
Ckers Finance	NBFC	✓	✓
Edelweiss Financial Services	NBFC		✓
Electronica Finance	NBFC	✓	✓
Federal Bank	FI	✓	✓
HDFC Bank	FI		✓
ICICI Bank Limited	FI		✓
IDFC First Bank	FI		✓
IndusInd Bank	FI		✓
Indostar Capital Finance Limited	NBFC		✓
IREDA	NBFC	✓	✓
Citi Union Bank	FI		✓
Northern Arc	NBFC	✓	✓
PTC Financial Services Limited	FI		✓
Rev Fin	Fintech	✓	✓
Siemens Financial Services	NBFC	✓	✓
TATA Cleantech	NBFC	✓	✓
Yes Bank	FI	✓	✓

FI = financial institution, Fintech = financial technology, NBFC = nonbanking financial company.
Source: Primary consultation.

PARTICIPATING FINANCIAL INSTITUTIONS UNDER EXISTING AND PREVIOUS FINANCING SCHEMES

Private Sector Financial Institutions under the Partial Risk Sharing Facility

Participating Financial Institutions
Electronica Finance Limited
HDFC Bank Limited
IndusInd Bank Ltd
Tata Cleantech Capital Limited
The Federal Bank Limited
Yes Bank Limited

Member Lending Institutions under the Credit Guarantee Fund Trust for Micro and Small Enterprises (CGTMSE)

Private Sector Banks
Axis Bank Ltd.
Catholic Syrian Bank
City Union Bank
Development Credit Bank Ltd.
HDFC Bank Ltd.
ICICI Bank Ltd.
IDBC Bank Ltd.
IDFC First Bank Ltd.
IndusInd Bank Ltd.
Karnataka Bank Ltd.
Kotak Mahindra Bank Ltd.
Lakshmi Vilas Bank
Tamilnad Mercantile Bank Ltd.
The Dhanalakshmi Bank Ltd.
The Nainital Bank Ltd.
The Ratnakar Bank Ltd.

continued on next page

Table *continued*

Foreign Banks
Bank of Bahrain and Kuwait
Barclays Bank PLC
DBS Bank
Deutsche Bank
Standard Chartered Bank

Small Finance Banks
AU Small Finance Bank
Equitas Small Finance Bank Ltd.
ESAF Small Finance Bank Ltd.
Northeast Small Finance Bank
Ujjivan Small Finance Bank Ltd.

Scheduled Commercial Banks
Andhra Pradesh Mahesh Co-operative Urban Bank Ltd
Bombay Mercantile Co-operative Bank Ltd
Citizen Credit Co-operative Bank Ltd
Jalgaon Peoples Co-op Bank Ltd
New India Co-operative Bank Ltd
NKGSB Co-Operative Bank Ltd.
Nutan Nagarik Sahakari Bank Ltd.
Saraswat Co-operative Bank Ltd.
Surat Peoples Coop Bank Ltd
SVC Co-operative Bank Ltd
The Ahmedabad Mercantile Co-op Bank Ltd
The Kalupur Commercial Co-op Bank Ltd
TJSB Sahakari Bank Ltd.

Private Financial Institutions under the Partial Risk Guarantee Fund for Energy Efficiency (PRGFEE)

Participating Financial Institutions
IDFC Bank
South Indian Bank
Tata Cleantech Capital
YES Bank Limited

Financial Institutions under the Technology Upgradation Funding Scheme (TUFS) for the Textile Sector

Financial Institutions Under the TUF Scheme
AXIS Bank
Catholic Syrian Bank
City Union Bank
Development Credit Bank Ltd., Mumbai
Dhanalakshmi Bank Ltd.
EXIM Bank
Federal Bank
HDFC Bank
ICICI Bank
IDBI Bank
IFCI
Laxmi Vilas Bank
Nainital Bank Ltd
Ratnakar Bank Ltd.
South Indian Bank
Yes Bank Ltd.

Sources: Government of India, Ministry of Textiles. Technology Upgradation Fund Scheme.

FINANCIAL INSTITUTIONS SHORT-LISTED FOR CONSULTATIONS

There were 21 financial institutions short-listed based on their prior financing history, sectors of focus, and overall expertise in the energy efficiency and climate smart infrastructure financing domain (Table A10).

Table A10: List of Financial Institutions with Experience

S. No.	Name	Type	Experience in Climate, Energy Efficiency, Climate-Smart Infrastructure, E-mobility, Climate Change Mitigation
1	Axis Bank	Private Bank	Sustainable lending
2	Akasa Finance	NBFC	Electric mobility
3	Caspian Impact Investments	NBFC	Clean energy, energy efficiency
4	Ckers Finance	NBFC	Clean energy, resource efficiency
5	Edelweiss Financial Services	NBFC	Clean energy and SME lending
6	Electronica Finance	NBFC	Energy efficiency in MSME, rooftop solar, climate finance
7	HSBC Bank	Private Bank	ESCO financing and demand-side management initiatives
8	ICICI Bank Limited	Private Bank	Energy efficiency, sustainable financing (renewable energy)
9	IDFC First Bank	Private Bank	PRSF/PRGFEE
10	IndoStar Capital Finance Limited	NBFC	Commercial vehicles and electric mobility
11	IndusInd Bank	Private Bank	PRSF/PRGFEE
12	Investment and Finance Company Limited	NBFC	Commercial vehicles and electric mobility
13	IREDA	NBFC	Renewable energy, energy efficiency
14	Kotak Mahindra Bank	Private Bank	Energy efficiency, renewable purchase obligation
15	L&T Infrastructure Finance	NBFC	Solar and wind energy projects
16	Northern Arc	NBFC	Electric mobility
17	PTC Financial Services Limited	Private Bank	PRSF/PRGFEE
18	Siemens Financial Services	NBFC	Energy transition
19	Stride Ventures	NBFC	Electric mobility
20	TATA Cleantech	NBFC	Clean-tech solutions, sustainable strategy development
21	Yes Bank	Private Bank	ESCO financing

ESCO = energy service company; MSME = micro, small, and medium-sized enterprise; NBFC = nonbanking financial company; PRGFEE = Partial Risk Guarantee Fund for Energy Efficiency; PRSF = partial risk sharing facility; SME = small and medium-sized enterprise.
Source: From consultation carried out by PwC.

9 789292 708436